SIMPLY ITALIAN

EASY RECIPES
THAT ARE QUICK TO PREPARE
AND LOW IN CALORIES

VALENTINA HARRIS

CB

CONTEMPORARY BOOKS

A TRIBUNE COMPANY

Library of Congress Cataloging-in-Publication Data

Harris, Valentina.
    Simply Italian : easy recipes that are quick to prepare and low
in calories / Valentina Harris.
        p.   cm.
    ISBN 0-8092-3040-2
    1. Cookery, Italian.   2. Quick and easy cookery.   3. Low-
fat diet—Recipes.   I. Title.
TX723.H3313   1996
641.5945—dc20   96-36602
                                      CIP

Cover design by Kim Bartko
Cover photograph by Martin Brigdale
Interior design by Grahame Dudley Associates
Interior photographs by Martin Brigdale

Featured on cover: Roasted Peppers, page 156

This edition is published by arrangement with BBC Worldwide
Americas Inc.

Copyright © 1995 by Valentina Harris
All rights reserved
Published by Contemporary Books
An imprint of NTC/Contemporary Publishing Company
Two Prudential Plaza, Chicago, Illinois 60601-6790
International Standard Book Number: 0-8092-3040-2
10   9   8   7   6   5   4   3   2   1

ACKNOWLEDGMENTS
I want to thank Suzanne Webber at BBC Books for the opportunity to
write this book, and my agent, Felicity Bryan, with whom I now
share ten years of books.

DEDICATION
For Sara and Pia, with whom I taste Italy

NOTES TO THE AMERICAN EDITION

Some of the recipes contain certain readily available ingredients whose names as listed might not be familiar to the North American reader. The following list is a glossary of those ingredients:

aubergine	eggplant
bream	flounder, or any flaky whitefish
beetleaf	Swiss chard
beetroot	beets
borlotti beans	red kidney beans
caster sugar	powdered sugar
courgettes	zucchini
passata	sieved canned tomatoes (see page 7)
pine kernels	pine nuts
rocket	arugula

CONTENTS

INTRODUCTION

· · · · · · · · · · · · ·

In the course of travelling around the world teaching authentic Italian cookery to quite literally hundreds of people I have had the opportunity to talk to countless readers of my cookery books. The question which I am asked most often is this: 'Of all the books you have had published, which is the one which is most suitable for everyday, normal family cooking?'

This has been the inspiration for this book. I thought a lot about this simple request for a book containing really unpretentious, cheap and cheerful Italian food, so I went ahead and wrote it. Whilst writing it, I bore in mind the scenario of a family just like my own, sitting round a table and eating food that people of all ages can enjoy. The recipes in this book are mostly recipes that I repeatedly cook for my own family. This is not 'restaurant' food, nor is it dinner party food, it is just honest, basic eating. It is food which requires a minimum amount of time in the kitchen, is easy and not too expensive to shop for, and is not too rich or packed with calories and fats.

Italian food does not rely on historically famous chefs for its technique or philosophy. Throughout Italy's culinary development the creative mainstay has always been the same: Mamma standing in her kitchen making the most of the available ingredients and inventing countless delicious ways of nourishing her family. The main ingredients of Italian food have always been, and continue to be, love and care.

This begins with the process of procuring the ingredients. It is perfectly obvious that if you are going to cook simple food which uses few ingredients, then the most important thing is that those ingredients should be of the best possible quality. This does not mean expensive, in fact in many cases it means quite the opposite. What it does mean is that the ingredients should be selected carefully, and used whilst they are still fresh, particularly in the case of vegetables, fish, cheese and meat. An Italian housewife or househusband will prefer to shop on a daily basis, rather than weekly, fortnightly or monthly. Great care is taken in selecting ingredients, because this is where the food preparation itself begins. If you cook with good, fresh ingredients, your finished dish is much more likely to do you justice. Equally, because you are using good, fresh ingredients, you must take care to do them justice.

I like food that is as simple, humble and unpretentious as possible. I belong to the 'don't mess with it' school of cookery, and I passionately believe that good food is one of the basic necessities of life. As a teacher, I have come to understand that I have many similar-minded friends out there.

It is all very well and usually extremely enjoyable to go out to a restaurant and indulge in complex, structured food, but will your six-year-old enjoy it too? Is it the sort of food that you're going to be in the mood to eat after a long day at the office? Surely we all need the simplicity of home cooking, as well? On the other hand, it is most important to keep home cooking as stimulating and interesting as possible. In this book, I have attempted to do just that. I present you with recipes for food that hopefully everybody in your home will love to eat, whilst being just 'different' enough to be interesting without being too exotic.

The ritual of sitting down together around a table to enjoy both good food, and each others' company, is one of the most vital and lasting elements of Italian life. But it is a practice which, in many other countries, is all too quickly in danger of disappearing and one which I firmly believe in. I wish you many happy hours at your table.

Buon appetito!

Valentina, July 1994

NOTES ON THE RECIPES

1 Follow one set of measurements only, do not mix metric and Imperial.
2 Eggs are size 2.
3 Wash fresh produce before preparation.
4 Spoon measurements are level.
5 A tablespoon is 15 ml; a teaspoon is 5 ml.
6 Adjust seasoning and strongly flavoured ingredients, such as onions and garlic, to suit your own taste.
7 If you substitute dried for fresh herbs, use only half the amount specified.
8 You will notice I frequently refer to an ingredient called passata. For anyone who is still not sure what this is, it is sieved canned tomatoes, so that all the seeds and skins have been removed for you. It has a lovely thick, creamy texture which cooks quickly and smoothly. It is widely available in cartons, cans or glass bottles.
9 In all cases where I refer to olive oil as an ingredient, I would prefer you to use extra virgin olive oil. This is the first pressing of olive oil and has the lowest oleic acidity level. I realize, however, that it can be expensive to use, so ordinary olive oil can be used instead. It is a good idea to build up a store of olive oils of different varieties: richer olive oil for salads or for drizzling over things, and lighter oil for cooking, for example. Olive oil is also very good for deep-frying.

SOUPS

· · · · · · · · · · · · · · · ·

To open this chapter on soups, a word first about the most essential ingredient for any soup: stock. Good stock will make any soup taste better, and it will make a good soup taste magnificent. Making stock is very easy, all you need is a little time to cook it. When a stock is rather plain and not very special it is called brodino. A really good, strong-flavoured, full-bodied stock is more like a broth, and is called brodo. This chapter begins by giving four recipes for basic stocks. With these at your fingertips, you can go on to create some wonderful soups.

VEGETABLE STOCK

This is an excellent way of using up vegetables which have lost their freshness and are beginning to look a bit limp.

●

Makes about 900 ml ($1\frac{1}{2}$ pints)
2 carrots, quartered
1 large onion, halved
2 celery sticks, quartered
2 tomatoes, halved
2–3 cabbage leaves, quartered
2 pinches of salt
$\frac{1}{2}$ leek, whole
8 lettuce leaves, halved
about 1.2 litres (2 pints) cold water

●

METHOD

Clean and prepare all the vegetables, then place them in a stock pot. Add the salt and pour over the water. Bring to the boil slowly, then cover and simmer for about $1\frac{1}{2}$ hours. Remove from the heat and leave to cool completely, then strain into a bowl or large jug. Keep in the refrigerator for up to 5 days or in the freezer for about 2 months.

OVERLEAF: Easy Minestrone (see page 16). A dusting of freshly grated Parmesan and a drizzle of extra virgin olive oil are the only garnishes needed to finish off this classic soup.

CHICKEN STOCK

You should never waste the chicken carcass from your Sunday joint – it's perfect as a base for you to make your own chicken stock.

●

Makes about 900 ml ($1\frac{1}{2}$ pints)
1 cooked chicken carcass or $\frac{1}{2}$ raw chicken, jointed
1 onion, quartered
2 celery sticks, halved
2 carrots, halved
about 1.2 litres (2 pints) cold water
2 pinches of salt

●

METHOD

Place the chicken and vegetables in a stock pot, pour over the water and add the salt. Bring to the boil, then cover and simmer for about 2 hours. Remove from the heat and leave to cool completely, then strain into a bowl or large jug. Keep in the refrigerator for up to 4 days or in the freezer for about 7 weeks.

FISH STOCK

Use whiting, plaice, mackerel, cod, monkfish heads — anything your fishmonger will give you!

●

Makes about 900 ml ($1\frac{1}{2}$ pints)

6–7 raw or cooked fish heads of any fish

200 g (7 oz) assorted bones, skin, trimmings etc. from raw or cooked fish

1 medium leek, sliced

1 large celery stick, quartered

6 sprigs of fresh parsley

$\frac{1}{4}$ lemon

2 pinches of salt

about 1.2 litres (2 pints) cold water

●

METHOD

Put all the fish in a stock pot. Add all the vegetables and lemon. Add the salt and water. Stir together, cover and bring to the boil. Simmer gently for about $1\frac{1}{2}$ hours. Remove from the heat and leave to cool completely. When it is cold, strain into a bowl or large jug. It will keep in the refrigerator for about 2 days or in the freezer for about 4 weeks.

MEAT STOCK

•

Makes about 900 ml (1½ pints)
7 oz (200 g) leftover cooked or raw meat, or 4–5 medium sized pork
or beef bones
1 large onion, quartered
2 carrots, quartered
2 celery sticks, quartered
2 tomatoes, halved
2–3 sprigs of fresh parsley
2 pinches of salt
about 1.2 litres (2 pints) cold water

•

METHOD

Put the meat in the stock pot. Add the vegetables then the salt and water. Cover and bring to the boil, then simmer gently for about 2 hours. Skim off any foam which might form on the surface while the stock cooks. Remove from the heat and leave to cool completely, then strain into a bowl or large jug. Skim off any surface fat before storing in the refrigerator for up to 4 days or in the freezer for about 1 week.

STOCK TIP

When you have made your stock, pour it into an empty ice cube tray and freeze. Break the ice cubes into plastic bags and label according to the type of stock contained and remember to date them! Store the plastic bags in your freezer. Thus you will always have stock of the right type and in the required quantity to hand.

Many supermarkets now sell excellent fresh fish stock of every possible variety in cartons or tubs.

TOMATO SOUP

Minestra di Pomodoro

SERVES 6

The difficulty in making fresh tomato soup taste like Italian fresh tomato soup is that Italian tomatoes always have a special ingredient called sunshine which makes them taste so sweet and rich. To achieve the same effect without those luscious varieties of tomato, the trick is to add a little concentrated tomato purée, or for an even sweeter flavour a little sun-dried tomato paste.

●

1 kg (2¼ lb) ripe red tomatoes
1 large onion, quartered
2 celery sticks, quartered
2 carrots, quartered
salt and freshly milled black pepper
about 600 ml (1 pint) vegetable stock or water
1 teaspoon best quality concentrated tomato purée (optional)

TO SERVE
freshly grated Parmesan

●

METHOD

Put all the vegetables into a heavy-based pan and season with salt and pepper. Cover with the stock and place a lid on the pan. Bring to the boil then simmer gently for about 30 minutes until the vegetables have all completely fallen to pieces. Push through a food mill or liquidize and then strain. Pour the soup back into the pan, taste and season again, if necessary, with salt and pepper. Warm the soup and stir in the concentrated tomato purée if necessary. Allow the soup to boil gently without a lid until reduced enough to have a thicker texture. Serve warm with freshly grated Parmesan cheese.

EASY MINESTRONE

Minestrone Facile

S E R V E S   6

As the name suggests, Minestrone is a big soup which is designed to fill you up. Apart from the assorted vegetables, the real filling quality is provided by the beans and the pasta or rice which finish it off. I am delighted to see that fresh borlotti beans are now becoming much more widely available. Somehow they always taste more Italian than the dried or canned varieties! Cooking times for different beans may vary considerably.

•

200 g (7 oz) borlotti beans, fresh or dried
4 tablespoons olive oil
I onion, finely chopped
a handful of fresh flatleaf parsley, chopped
300 g (II oz) mixed green vegetables, such as
spinach, cabbage, Swiss chard, lettuce leaves or spring greens, chopped
2 courgettes, cubed
I potato, cubed
I carrot, cubed
200 g (7 oz) short stubby pasta or long-grain rice
salt and freshly milled black pepper

TO SERVE
olive oil
freshly grated Parmesan

•

M E T H O D

First, attend to the beans. If they are dried, soak them overnight in cold water, drain and rinse then boil fast in cold water for 5 minutes, then drain and rinse again. Dried or fresh, they then need to be placed in a large pan and just covered with fresh water or stock, brought to the boil then simmered gently for about 1 hour until tender but not falling apart. Drain, reserving the cooking liquid. Do not add salt to the water until the beans are tender as this will cause the skin to shrivel and harden.

Fry the onion gently in the olive oil until soft. Add the tender beans and stir rice together thoroughly. Then add the parsley, green vegetables, courgettes, potato and carrot. Fry together gently, using the water from the beans to moisten. When the vegetables are all beginning to soften, pour in the rest of the bean water to cover thoroughly, turn the heat down and simmer slowly for about 30 minutes, stirring regularly. Add more liquid if necessary, either from the beans or use vegetable stock or water. When the vegetables are thoroughly soft, season to taste with salt and pepper and add the pasta or rice. Cook gently for about 10–20 minutes until the pasta or rice is cooked, then transfer to warmed soup bowls or a tureen. Serve with a drizzle of olive oil and sprinkle over a little freshly grated Parmesan cheese.

CROSTINI FOR SOUP

Crostini da zuppa

SERVES 6

●

3–5 tablespoons olive oil
1 garlic clove, left whole and lightly crushed
5 slices ciabatta bread, cubed

●

METHOD

Heat the olive oil with the garlic in a wide frying pan until the garlic is golden, then toss in the bread. Fry quickly on all sides until golden and crisp. Drain carefully on kitchen paper and then transfer to a bowl until required.

EASY CHICK PEA SOUP

Zuppa di Ceci Facile

SERVES 6

This humble pulse takes on the flavour of the other components in a recipe with a minimum of fuss and bother. Soak the chick peas overnight, but for no more than 20 hours.

●

400 g (14 oz) chick peas
about 1.2 ml (2 pints) cold water or stock
1 tablespoon unsalted butter
1 onion, chopped
1 carrot, chopped
1 celery stick, chopped
175 g (6 oz) pancetta or streaky unsmoked bacon, rinded and
finely chopped
salt and freshly milled black pepper

TO SERVE
6 slices ciabatta bread, toasted
1 tablespoon butter
3 tablespoons freshly grated Parmesan

●

METHOD

Soak the chick peas overnight in cold water then drain, rinse, cover with the fresh water or stock and boil gently for about 1 hour. Do not add salt, as this will toughen them. When the chick peas are soft enough to be squashed completely when pressed against a surface with your thumb, drain and reserve the cooking liquid.

In a separate pan, fry the butter with the onion, carrot, celery and pancetta or bacon until the vegetables are softened. Add the chick peas and stir thoroughly, then pour in the liquid from the chick peas, stir well and season with salt and pepper. Bring to the boil, cover and simmer for about 1 hour until the chick peas are completely soft. Butter the toasted bread lightly and arrange on the bottom of a warmed soup tureen or individual bowls. Pour over the soup and serve sprinkled with a little freshly grated Parmesan cheese.

Easy Chick Pea Soup: a hint of butter, a touch of bacon and some tasty bread turn the simplest soup into something really special.

CAULIFLOWER SOUP

Zuppa di Cavolfiore

SERVES 6

Cauliflower soup can be one of the most boring soups of all. In this recipe, it is transformed into a delicious, garlic-laden delight. Removing the seeds from the chilli pepper will make the soup less spicy.

•

1 cauliflower, broken into small florets
about 1.2 litres (2 pints) cold water or stock
2 pinches of salt
4 tablespoons olive oil
3 garlic cloves, left whole
$\frac{1}{2}$ dried red chilli pepper

TO SERVE
2–3 tablespoons extra virgin olive oil
freshly grated Pecorino

•

METHOD

Boil the cauliflower gently in the water or stock with the salt for about 5 minutes until barely tender. Meanwhile, heat the olive oil and fry the garlic and chilli together until the garlic is golden. Drain the cauliflower, reserving the cooking water. Tip the cauliflower into the pan with the garlic and fry gently together for a few minutes until the cauliflower has absorbed almost all the oil. Add the water and stir. Simmer gently for about 15 minutes until the cauliflower has almost completely fallen apart. Discard the garlic and chilli. Transfer to a soup tureen or individual bowls. Drizzle the surface with a little olive oil and sprinkle with freshly grated Pecorino cheese and serve at once.

VEGETABLE SOUP

Zuppa di Verdura

SERVES 6

*This is the soup I was brought up on, and which I have gone on to bring up all my children on!
The type of vegetables can vary according to availability and season, but the important thing is
to have lots and lots of different kinds. For a 'leaner' soup, leave out the eggs and milk.*

●

1.5 kg (3½ lb) mixed fresh vegetables such as carrots, cabbage, courgettes,
turnips, potatoes, spinach, celery and onion
about 300 ml (10 fl oz) vegetable or chicken stock
salt and freshly milled black pepper
3 eggs, beaten
3 tablespoons hot milk

TO SERVE
Crostini for Soup (see page 17)
freshly grated Parmesan

●

METHOD

Clean and chop all the vegetables coarsely. Place in a pan and cover with the stock.
Bring to the boil, cover and simmer gently for 20–30 minutes until completely soft.
Push through a sieve or liquidize and then strain. Season with salt and pepper. Whisk
in the eggs and milk and transfer to a warmed soup tureen or individual bowls. Serve
at once with Crostini and freshly grated Parmesan cheese.

EASY BEAN SOUP

Zuppa di Fagioli Facile

S E R V E S   6

This basic bean soup is simplicity itself, but it really needs the flavour of fresh borlotti beans to make it outstanding. However, even with dried beans it is delicious. The magical finishing touch is a tablespoon or two of the finest, most wickedly rich olive oil and some freshly milled black pepper. The natural salinity of the celery makes it especially wonderful and extra healthy!

●

200 g (7 oz) fresh or dried borlotti beans
about 1.2 litres (2 pints) cold water or stock
175 g (6 oz) celery sticks, coarsely chopped
extra virgin olive oil
freshly milled back pepper

●

M E T H O D

Soak dried beans overnight in cold water then drain and rinse thoroughly. Cover the soaked, dried beans or fresh beans with the fresh water or stock and slowly bring to the boil. Cover and simmer gently for about 45 minutes until half cooked, then add the celery. Stir thoroughly, return to the boil then continue to simmer for a further 1 hour. When the beans are almost pulpy and the celery has practically vanished into the soup, pour the soup into a warmed tureen or individual bowls. Drizzle with a little olive oil, sprinkle with the freshly milled black pepper and serve at once.

Easy Bean Soup: the only finishing touch needed for this nourishing soup is a generous turn of the pepper mill.

POTATO SOUP

Minestra di Patate

SERVES 6

The humble potato makes a deliciously filling, simple soup for winter evenings. You can vary the type of herbs used if you like, but every time I taste the marriage of the flavours of rosemary and potatoes together, I am more convinced than ever that they were made for each other!

●

4 fist-sized potatoes, cubed
1 onion, thinly sliced
5 tablespoons olive oil
2–3 sprigs of fresh rosemary or $\frac{1}{2}$ teaspoon dried rosemary
about 1.2 litres (2 pints) chicken or vegetable stock
salt and freshly milled black pepper

●

METHOD

Fry the potatoes and onion together very gently in the olive oil with the rosemary, just until the onion is slightly softened. If the potato looks like it is browning, add a few spoonfuls of chicken stock to keep well moistened. Once the onion is soft, pour in the remaining stock and stir thoroughly. Cover and bring to the boil, reduce the heat and simmer gently for about 15 minutes until the potatoes are soft. Taste the soup and add salt and freshly milled black pepper as necessary. Remove and discard the rosemary. Pour the soup into a warmed tureen or individual bowls and serve.

CLEAR CHICKEN SOUP WITH PASTINA

Pastina in Brodo

SERVES 6

Every nationality has its own version of 'comfort food', those delectable things which we eat in order to cheer ourselves up, the sort of things which remind us of our childhood. The ultimate Italian comfort food is Pastina in Brodo: baby pasta cooked in best quality, full-flavoured stock. The shape of the pasta you choose – be it stars, rings, little tubes, flowers or whatever – is entirely up to how you feel at the time. You'll need about a handful per person.

It is quite common for this soup to be served as a family first course at supper time at least once a week, all over Italy. In serving the soup, you should take into account who likes more stock and less pasta or vice versa. In Italy you will be asked whether you want it bagnata *(wet) or* asciutta *(dry).*

●

about 1.5 litres (3 pints) best quality chicken stock (brodo)
about 350 g (12 oz) baby pasta of your choice

TO SERVE
freshly grated Parmesan

●

METHOD

Bring the stock to the boil and then trickle in the pastina. Stir and continue to boil for 5–10 minutes until the pastina is tender. Pour into a warmed soup tureen or individual bowls and serve at once, offering freshly grated Parmesan separately.

RED ONION SOUP

Zuppa di Cipolle Rosse

SERVES 6

*(unless you have a cold, in which case you need
to eat it all yourself in the course of the day)*

*This is one of the many recipes that the French claim to have created, but which Italians (in
this particular case the cooks of the Como district) say is theirs. Whoever invented the soup, it
is absolutely perfect for a cold day and my mother says it is the best possible cure for a bad cold,
especially if you wash it down with plenty of heady red wine. After that, go straight to sleep and
hopefully you'll wake up feeling much better! If you don't want to make your own bouquet garni,
use a good quality, ready-made one from the delicatessen or supermarket.*

•

120 g (4½ oz) unsalted butter
1.5 kg (3 lb) red onions, very thinly sliced
about 900 ml (1½ pints) best quality stock (brodo)
1 bouquet garni (a sprig of fresh rosemary, a sprig of fresh thyme,
a sprig of fresh sage, 2 sprigs of fresh parsley, and a bay leaf,
tied together in a bunch with cook's string)
salt and freshly milled black pepper
6 thick slices ciabatta bread, toasted

•

METHOD

Put a little butter to one side to spread on the toast. Fry the onions incredibly slowly in a very heavy-based pan with the butter. The onions must melt into the butter
without browning at all, so this will take at least 20 minutes. Pour over the stock,
just to cover the onions, and add the bunch of herbs. Cover and simmer gently for
about 20 minutes or until the soup has thickened. Season to taste. Butter the toast
and place the slices in the bottom of a warmed soup tureen or individual bowls.
Discard the bunch of herbs, pour the hot soup over the bread and serve at once.

Red Onion Soup: this really is pretty enough to eat. It's also a foolproof cure for colds.

RICE
AND RISOTTO

• • • • • • • • • • • • • •

Rice dishes and risotto form a very important part of the Italian diet. There are so many different recipes: literally hundreds of thick soups, baked rice dishes, rice salads and risottos. Rice has been part of the Italian diet in some form or another ever since the Arabs introduced rice into Sicily in the eighth century. It is without question as much a part of the Italian food scene as pasta. Here are just a few examples of some of the best loved family recipes for using rice. In terms of ingredients, in many cases you'll need to use stock, for which you will need to refer back to the previous chapter. The rice itself is the other major ingredient, and I am thrilled to see risotto rice appearing on virtually every supermarket shelf these days. More specialized, regional, varieties of rice (such as Vialone Nano, Roma, Originario) are available from the better Italian delicatessens and larger supermarkets.

RISOTTO WITH PARSLEY

Risottino al Prezzemolo

SERVES 6

This way of cooking a risotto is very different to the classical method of frying the rice in oil and butter, then gradually adding the stock and the other ingredients (such as mushrooms, seafood, game, sausages or whatever), allowing the rice to swell and soften. In fact, this method is a much older version than the frying version, and it is a bit lower in calories and fat too!

●

about 1.5 litres (2½ pints) best quality chicken,
vegetable or meat stock (brodo)
300 g (11 oz) Arborio or other risotto rice
400 g (14 oz) flatleaf parsley (weigh with stalks),
stalks removed and finely chopped
1 tablespoon unsalted butter
2–3 tablespoons freshly grated Parmesan
salt and freshly milled black pepper

TO SERVE
freshly grated Parmesan

●

METHOD

Bring the stock to the boil, trickle in the rice and stir. Simmer for about 20 minutes until the rice has absorbed nearly all the stock and is soft and creamy. Stir in the parsley, butter and cheese. Taste and season with salt and pepper. Cover and rest for about 2 minutes, then pour into a warmed tureen or individual bowls and serve at once with more grated cheese offered separately.

RICE AND PUMPKIN

Riso e Zucca

SERVES 6

The best pumpkins are firm and ripe with no trace of bruising. This dish is a cross between a risotto and a soup. It has a lovely bright orange colour, perfect for warming a winter's evening.

•

400 g (14 oz) yellow pumpkin, peeled and seeded
1 onion, chopped
1 carrot, chopped
1 celery stick, chopped
6 tablespoons olive oil
about 1.5 litres (3 pints) chicken or vegetable stock
300 g (11 oz) Arborio or other risotto rice
salt and freshly milled black pepper
3–4 tablespoons freshly grated Parmesan

•

METHOD

Trim and chop the pumpkin. Fry the onion, carrot and celery together with the olive oil until softened, then add the pumpkin and continue to cook for about 5 minutes until the pumpkin is also slightly softened. Pour in the stock, bring to the boil and simmer for about 5 minutes until the pumpkin is cooked. Add the rice and continue to simmer for about 20 minutes until the rice is also cooked. Remove from the heat and season to taste with salt and pepper, then stir in the cheese and cover. Leave to stand for about 5 minutes before serving.

Rice and Pumpkin: ripe pumpkin gives this delicious risotto a marvellous colour, texture and flavour.

RICE AND CABBAGE

Riso e Verze

SERVES 6

This is a really old, very traditional dish from Italy's cucina povera. Like all dishes which use very few basic ingredients, it is important that they should be of the best possible quality. The oil should be really rich, deep and green, with plenty of flavour to match its good looks.

●

1 very large onion, chopped
5 tablespoons olive oil
1 large celery stick, chopped
600 g (1¼ lb) green cabbage leaves, shredded
about 1.5 litres (2½ pints) chicken, vegetable or meat stock, kept boiling hot
300 g (11 oz) risotto rice
salt and freshly milled black pepper
4–5 tablespoons freshly grated Parmesan

●

METHOD

Fry the onion in the olive oil over a gentle heat until soft then add the celery and cabbage. Fry together for about 5 minutes, then pour in the boiling stock, stir and simmer until all the vegetables are completely tender. Stir in the rice and simmer for about 20 minutes until tender. Taste and season with salt and pepper then stir in the cheese. Cover and leave to stand for about 5 minutes before serving.

RICE AND PEAS

Risi e Bisi

SERVES 6

This deliciously creamy Venetian dish is another one of those rice dishes which is a cross between a risotto and a soup. There are many different versions of this dish. For perfect results, you should really use fresh peas and make a stock with the empty pods, which is then used to cook the rice. If this proves too difficult and you must use frozen peas, make sure they are of the best quality and use either vegetable or chicken stock.

●

450 g (1 lb) fresh peas (shelled weight)
2 tablespoons olive oil
2 onions, finely chopped
2 celery sticks, chopped
1–2 garlic cloves, finely chopped
300 g (11 oz) Arborio or other risotto rice
about 1.5 litres (2½ pints) vegetable, chicken or
pea pod stock, kept boiling hot
1 tablespoon unsalted butter or 2 tablespoons olive oil
salt and freshly milled black pepper
4 tablespoons freshly grated Parmesan

●

METHOD

Fry the peas slowly with the olive oil, onions, celery and garlic for about 5 minutes. Then add the rice and stir together for about 5 minutes before gradually adding the hot stock, one or two ladles full at a time, stirring frequently. This process will take about 15 minutes and you will need to keep all the ingredients in a semi-liquid state, stirring constantly. When the rice is cooked, take off the heat and stir in the butter or olive oil. Taste and season with salt and pepper then stir in the cheese and cover. Leave to stand for about 3 minutes, then transfer to a warmed dish and serve.

RISOTTO WITH COURGETTES

Risotto di Zucchine

SERVES 6

A very simple classic, full of flavour and with plenty of interesting texture, this risotto is cooked using the frying method, gradually absorbing stock as it cooks.

●

40 g (1½ oz) pancetta or streaky bacon, rinded and chopped
2 tablespoons olive oil
1 onion, finely chopped
450 g (1 lb) tender courgettes, finely cubed
300 (11 oz) Arborio or other risotto rice
about 1.5 litres (2½ pints) chicken or vegetable stock, kept boiling hot
3 tablespoons finely chopped fresh parsley
salt and freshly milled black pepper
4 tablespoons freshly grated Parmesan

●

METHOD

Fry the pancetta or bacon, olive oil and onion together until the onion is softened. Add the courgettes and fry together for about 5 minutes, stirring constantly. Add the rice and toast the grains all over. Add a ladle full of hot stock, stir in into the rice and continue to cook the rice in this way: add a little stock, stir until the rice has absorbed the liquid, then add more. It will take about 20 minutes for the rice to become creamy and tender. When the rice is cooked through, take off the heat and stir in the parsley. Taste and season with salt and pepper. Stir in the cheese, cover and leave to stand for about 5 minutes before serving.

Risotto with Courgettes: pancetta and courgettes are a perfect partnership for this wonderful risotto.

MUSHROOM RISOTTO

Risotto con i Funghi

SERVES 6

Probably one of the most popular of all the classic risotti can be made with your favourite mushrooms, although the flavour is best enhanced with the addition of a few dried porcini.

●

1 onion, finely chopped
2 tablespoons chopped fresh parsley
1 garlic clove, chopped
2 tablespoons unsalted butter
25 g (1 oz) dried porcini mushrooms, soaked in warm water for
about 20 minutes, then drained and liquid reserved
350 g (12 oz) Arborio or other risotto rice
1.5 litres (2½ pints) chicken or vegetable stock, kept boiling hot
200 g (7 oz) cultivated or wild mushrooms, sliced
2 tablespoons freshly grated Parmesan

●

METHOD

Fry the onion, parsley and garlic together with half the butter until soft. Dry the soaked mushrooms carefully then chop them coarsely. Add to the other ingredients. Stir thoroughly and then add the rice and fry until dry but without letting the rice brown. Begin to add the stock gradually, letting the rice absorb the stock before adding any more. After about 10 minutes when the rice is half cooked, add the reserved liquid from the soaked mushrooms, and the sliced mushrooms. Continue to add the stock and stir until the rice is soft and tender and the mushrooms are cooked through. Remove from the heat and stir in the remaining butter and the Parmesan. Cover and leave to stand for about 4 minutes then transfer to a warmed serving dish and serve at once.

RICE AND LENTILS

Riso e Lenticchie

S E R V E S   6

This is one of the most evocative flavours of my life as a child growing up in Italy. It reminds me so poignantly of those first cold autumn evenings after the day had been spent outside, taking care of the olive groves and vineyards before winter set in. Our appetites were sharp in those days, thanks to the fresh air and hard work, and every time I taste Riso e Lenticchie it brings back all those feelings.

●

300 g (11 oz) small green or brown lentils
3 onions, finely chopped
4 tablespoons olive oil
about 1.5 litres (3 pints) chicken, meat or vegetable stock
salt and freshly milled black pepper
300 g (11 oz) Arborio or other risotto rice

●

M E T H O D

Soak the lentils in plenty of cold water overnight or for up to 20 hours. Skim off all the lentils which have risen to the surface and discard them. Place in a pan, cover with fresh water and boil the lentils very fast for about 5 minutes, then drain and rinse. Set aside until required.

Fry the onions gently in the olive oil until they are completely softened. Tip in the lentils and stir. Cover generously with the stock and season to taste with salt and pepper. Simmer for about 35 minutes or until the lentils are tender, then add the rice. Stir and simmer until the rice is tender. Take off the heat, check and adjust the seasoning with salt and pepper and transfer into a warmed bowl to serve.

TOMATO RISOTTO

Risotto ai Pomodori

SERVES 6 GENEROUSLY

Instead of tomato, you could vary this risotto by adding aubergines, peppers, or maybe even a combination of all three! Very easy to make, it is also tasty and filling.

●

400 g (14 oz) fresh tomatoes
2–3 garlic cloves, very finely chopped
4 tablespoons olive oil
400 g (14 oz) risotto rice
about 1.5 litres (2½ pints) vegetable, meat or chicken stock, kept boiling hot
2–3 tablespoons chopped fresh parsley
salt and freshly milled black pepper

●

METHOD

Dip all the tomatoes in boiling water for about 1 minute, then skin them quickly. Cut them in half and take out the seeds. Chop the tomatoes very coarsely. Fry the garlic gently in the olive oil for about 5 minutes. Add the rice and dry out the rice carefully, then add one ladle full of stock and stir. Continue to add stock, wait for the rice to absorb the liquid and then add more stock. Stir continuously while you cook the risotto, which must remain just wet enough to ripple while it cooks. It will take about 20 minutes for the rice to cook through.

When the rice is half cooked, stir in the tomatoes and the parsley. When the rice is completely tender, remove from the heat and season to taste with salt and pepper. Cover and allow to rest for about 2 minutes. Transfer to a warmed platter and serve.

Tomato Risotto: the secret of this risotto is to use the ripest, sweetest tomatoes and the most fragrant herbs.

PASTA

· · · · · · · · · · · · ·

This quintessential Italian ingredient has become one of the most popular food-stuffs the world has ever known. There are quite literally hundreds of different pasta shapes, and many thousands of wonderful dressings and sauces to go with them. Once you have mastered the idea of boiling and draining pasta, putting a sauce over it and tossing them together, there is really no limit to what you can decide to put on to pasta if you so wish. Remember there is a definite relationship between the shape of pasta you choose to cook and the sauce or dressing which goes with it. The idea is that when you finish eating the dish, there should be only a little bit of the sauce left in the plate, so the shape of pasta chosen needs to have the ability to embrace and gather up as much of whatever is dressing it as you eat, rather than falling off. So as a very general rule, choose smooth sauces with long pasta shapes and lumpy sauces with short and stubby shapes. But having said that, the exceptions to the rule are so many as to make it almost useless! And many people only like one shape and refuse to eat any other, no matter what the sauce is!

There are two basic types of pasta which are widely available everywhere. The first is dried durum wheat pasta, consisting of durum wheat flour and water, mixed, cut and dried in factory conditions. This is the pasta you cannot make at home and includes spaghetti, bucatini, penne, fusilli and about six hundred other shapes. Fresh pasta is made with ordinary flour and eggs, kneaded together to make a much softer, richer, more luxurious pasta. This can be made at home and includes tagliatelle, fettuccine, cannelloni, lasagne and many others.

Dried durum wheat pasta in itself is very good for you and not as fatten-ing as one might think. A plate of durum wheat spaghetti dressed with a very basic and simple tomato, olive oil, garlic and basil sauce contains just under 300 calories. With a fat-free sauce like the one on page 44, the calories are even fewer. Of course, a plate of pasta covered in a creamy, butter-filled, alcohol-laden sauce is packed with calories and all sorts of other extras that are not so good if you are watching your diet. In fact, recent research has shown that some pasta dishes are so clogged with cream, butter and cheese that they actually contain more calories and fat than a huge slab of chocolate cake. The moral of the tale is: be careful what you put on the pasta, but most of all – enjoy it!

THE SECRETS OF SUCCESSFUL PASTA

1 Plenty of water for the pasta to move around freely while it cooks. Ideally you need 1 litre ($1\frac{3}{4}$ pints) of water per 100 g (4 oz) of pasta. You should not need to add oil to the water in order to prevent the pasta from sticking unless you really do not have enough water in the pot.

2 Use 6–10 g (1–2 teaspoons) of salt per litre ($1\frac{3}{4}$ pints) of water, depending on how savoury or flavoursome your sauce or dressing is going to be. So, always make sure the water is salted accurately!

3 Don't even think about putting your pasta into the salted water until it has achieved a rolling boil.

4 Drain the pasta as soon as it is cooked to the point when you as the cook feel it is ready – the only way to tell is to fish a bit out and taste it. Times vary considerably, but as a guide, fresh pasta will take 3–5 minutes and dried pasta 5–10 minutes.

5 Once drained, dress the pasta at once and serve as soon as possible. Remember that the pasta continues cooking even once out of the pan, so while the pasta cooks get yourself ready to drain, dress and generally prepare it for the table. Only in very rare cases is a little residual water useful for loosening or diluting your sauce. Usually it is best to drain all the water thoroughly from the pasta.

OVERLEAF: Fat-free Tomato Sauce (see page 44). A family classic which needs really ripe tomatoes.

PASTA WITH FAT-FREE TOMATO SAUCE

Pasta con Salsa al Pomodoro senza Grassi

SERVES 6

This is a lovely sauce to serve over your favourite shape of pasta containing nothing but fresh vegetables. If you want to (and if your calorie counting permits!) you can add a little butter or olive oil at the very end when you toss everything together.

●

750 g (1½ lb) fresh ripe tomatoes
1 large celery stick, quartered
1 large carrot, quartered
1 large onion, quartered
7–8 sprigs of fresh basil
7–8 sprigs of fresh parsley including stalks
450 g (1 lb) pasta of your choice
salt and freshly milled black pepper (optional)
1–2 tablespoons olive oil or unsalted butter (optional)
freshly grated Parmesan (optional)

●

METHOD

Place all the vegetables and herbs into a pan which is not too wide and deep. Cover and place over a low heat. Allow all the vegetables to exude their own juices and simmer slowly together until pulpy, shaking the pan occasionally. Then cool and push through a food mill or sieve (alternatively you can whizz in the processor, then push it through a sieve). The result will be a fairly liquid sauce (more like soup) which you will need to reduce until thickened. To do this, simply put the pan over a medium heat and let the sauce boil quickly without burning. Keep an eye on the sauce and take it off the heat when you feel the consistency is about right.

Cook the pasta in plenty of boiling salted water, then drain and dress with the reduced sauce. Add salt and freshy milled black pepper, olive oil or butter and Parmesan to taste.

PASTA WITH SUN-DRIED TOMATOES

Pasta con Pomodori Secchi

SERVES 4–6

This delicious mixture of fresh and sun-dried tomatoes makes a lovely sweet-flavoured sauce that is perfect with any shape of pasta.

●

5–6 tablespoons olive oil
1 small onion, finely chopped
1 celery stick, finely chopped
225 g (8 oz) sun-dried tomatoes preserved in olive oil, coarsely chopped
300 g (11 oz) fresh ripe tomatoes, skinned, seeded and coarsely chopped
freshly milled black pepper
450 g (1 lb) dried durum wheat pasta of your choice
(spaghetti, penne etc.)
2 tablespoons chopped fresh flatleaf parsley

●

METHOD

Fry together the olive oil, onion and celery until the vegetables are soft. Add the sun-dried tomatoes and fry together very gently for a further 5–10 minutes, then add the fresh tomatoes. Stir, cover and simmer slowly for about 20 minutes or until the sauce is thickened and glossy.

Bring a large pan of salted water to the boil. Tip in the pasta, stir and return to the boil. When the pasta is ready, drain quickly and return to the pan it was cooked in. Pour over the sauce, toss together thoroughly and add the pepper. Toss again, then tip out on to a warmed platter, into a warmed pasta bowl, or on to individual plates. Sprinkle with the parsley and serve immediately.

PASTA WITH A GARLIC, TOMATO AND BASIL SAUCE

Pasta con Pomodoro, Aglio e Basilico

SERVES 6

Delightfully fresh and easy to make, especially since basil has become so easy to buy in its fresh form. I hope that soon we will be able to buy deliciously juicy fresh garlic all over the world too. The difference between fresh and old garlic is really quite remarkable.

•

2 garlic cloves, thinly sliced or crushed
3 tablespoons olive oil
400 g (14 oz) canned tomatoes or passata
about 9 leaves fresh basil, torn into small pieces with your fingers
salt and freshly milled black pepper
450 g (1 lb) pasta of your choice

TO SERVE
freshly grated Parmesan or Pecorino

•

METHOD

Fry the garlic very gently with the olive oil in a heavy-based pan or frying pan. When the garlic is soft, pour in the tomatoes and stir carefully. Cover and simmer for about 20 minutes or until the sauce is glossy and thick. Then add the basil and stir. Season to taste with salt and pepper and cover. Remove from the heat and keep warm.

Bring a large pan of salted water to a rolling boil, add the pasta and return to the boil, stirring. Drain the pasta as soon as it is cooked, return it to the pan and pour over the warm sauce. Toss everything together and transfer on to a warmed platter. Serve at once, with freshly grated Parmesan or Pecorino offered separately.

Pasta with a Garlic, Tomato and Basil Sauce: a really fast and foolproof pasta sauce.

PASTA WITH PESTO

Pasta al Pesto

SERVES 6

There are so many different recipes for this very important Ligurian sauce that I approach the subject with some concern in case you find this either repetitive or just plain boring! However, in truth, no collection of simple, basic recipes could be complete without including another version. This one works on the basis of pesto needing six large leaves of basil per person, that is 100 g (4 oz) per serving. The amount of garlic required is largely up to personal taste, although its complete exclusion will mean this sauce is no longer a pesto but simply a basil sauce.

●

36 large leaves fresh basil
3 cloves of garlic at least, more if desired
2–3 tablespoons freshly grated Parmesan or Pecorino
2–3 tablespoons pine kernels
50–75 ml (2–3 fl oz) best quality olive oil
1 tablespoon cooked, chopped spinach (optional)
salt and freshly milled black pepper
450 g (1 lb) fresh trenette or dried durum wheat bavette or linguine

TO SERVE
freshly grated Parmesan

●

METHOD

Ideally, this whole process should take place in a pestle and mortar, but if you do not have the inclination for such an intensive labour of love, then a food processor will just have to do! Process or pound all the basil leaves together with the garlic, Parmesan, pine kernels and olive oil. You should end up with a beautifully green, relatively smooth sauce with a bit of crunch. If you want an even greener sauce, add the spinach, if using. This will add depth and intensity to the sauce's colour and texture and season to taste. Bring a large pan of salted water to the boil. Add the pasta and return to the boil. Cook until tender, then drain thoroughly. Return to the hot pan and pour over the cold pesto. Toss together thoroughly, then transfer to a warmed platter. Serve with freshly grated Parmesan cheese offered separately.

PASTA WITH A FISH SAUCE

Pasta al Sugo di Pesce

SERVES 6

I like to use a fish that can withstand a fairly long cooking time without losing all its flavour and texture, so I have opted for a thick swordfish steak, chopped into small cubes, and some white fish which will flake better. In this way, there are two completely separate textures within the same dish. However you can use any combination of fish of your choice, or even use squid if you prefer. Cheese is never served with fish pasta dishes, or at least, extremely rarely.

●

3 tablespoons olive oil
2 garlic cloves, thinly sliced
2–3 tablespoons chopped fresh parsley
$\frac{1}{4}$ dried red chilli pepper
1 swordfish steak, cubed
2 cod fillets, cubed
2–3 tablespoons dry white wine
300 ml (10 fl oz) passata
salt and freshly milled black pepper
450 g (1 lb) pasta of your choice
2 tablespoons chopped fresh mint

●

METHOD

Fry the olive oil, garlic, parsley and chilli together very slowly, then add all the fish and fry together for about 3 minutes. Add the wine and stir for about 2 minutes to boil off the alcohol, then add the passata. Stir together thoroughly and season to taste with salt and pepper. Cover and simmer for about 15 minutes or until the sauce is thick and glossy.

Bring a large pan of salted water to the boil, then add the pasta. Return to the boil and cook until tender, then drain and return to the pan. Pour over the sauce, sprinkle with the mint and toss everything together very thoroughly. Then transfer to a warmed serving platter and serve immediately.

PASTA WITH COURGETTES

Pasta e Zucchine

SERVES 6

The lovely sweet flavour of courgettes is perfect with pasta in a simple dressing like this. It could not be easier to make and is surprisingly tasty (considering how few ingredients it contains); it really is packed with flavour. Secrets for maximum success are: fresh, best quality courgettes and very tasty olive oil.

●

200 g (7 oz) tender courgettes, sliced into discs
120 ml (4 fl oz) olive oil
salt and freshly milled black pepper
450 g (1 lb) pasta of your choice

TO SERVE
freshly grated Parmesan

●

METHOD

Fry the courgettes gently in a very large frying pan with the olive oil until browned around the edges and softened. Season to taste with salt and pepper. Bring a large pan of salted water to the boil and tip in the pasta. Stir and return to the boil. When the pasta is cooked, drain it and transfer it into the frying pan with the courgettes and olive oil. Toss the pasta and courgettes quickly together over a medium heat, then tip it all on to a warmed platter and serve with freshly grated Parmesan cheese offered separately.

Pasta with Courgettes: what could be simpler – or more delicious!

PASTA WITH MUSHROOM AND TUNA SAUCE

Pasta alla Boscaiola

SERVES 6

One of the ever-popular sauces is this classic tomato sauce with tuna and mushrooms. The nice thing about it is that you can leave out either the tuna or the mushrooms and still have a delicious sauce for your pasta.

•

200 g (7 oz) fresh mushrooms, sliced
4–5 tablespoons olive oil
100 g (4 oz) canned tuna in olive oil
salt and freshly milled black pepper
3 garlic cloves, crushed
450 g (1 lb) canned or fresh tomatoes, skinned, seeded and coarsely chopped
450 g (1 lb) pasta of your choice
1–3 tablespoons chopped fresh parsley

•

METHOD

Fry together the mushrooms and half the olive oil until the mushrooms are tender. Add the tuna and stir together, flaking the fish. Season with plenty of salt and pepper. In a separate pan, fry the garlic with the remaining oil until the garlic is golden brown, then add the tomatoes. Stir and season with salt and pepper, then leave to simmer until required.

Bring a large pan of salted water to the boil, add the pasta and stir. Return to the boil and cook until tender, then drain thoroughly and return to the pan. Add the tomato sauce and mix the pasta and sauce together thoroughly. Then add the mushrooms and tuna and the parsley. Mix together again. Transfer to a warmed platter and serve at once.

PASTA WITH YELLOW PEPPER SAUCE

Pasta al Peperone Giallo

SERVES 6

This is a lovely sauce that can be made in the food processor and then tipped over piping hot pasta. I owe this very original and efficient method of taking the outer skin off the peppers to Gerry Goldwyre, the Masterchef winner of 1994. So impressed was I that I have prepared my peppers like this ever since!

●

2 large juicy yellow peppers
1 egg
1 garlic clove
3 tablespoons chopped fresh parsley
3 tablespoons olive oil
salt and freshly milled black pepper
450 g (1 lb) pasta of your choice

TO SERVE
freshly grated Parmesan

●

METHOD

Roast the peppers either under the grill, in the oven or with a blow torch or lit gas ring until the exterior is blackened. Wrap them tightly in cling film and leave them to cool. Meanwhile, bring a large pan of salted water to a rolling boil. When the peppers are cool, rub off their exterior skin with a clean scouring pad, holding the peppers under a cold running tap. If you do this carefully and you have blackened the peppers efficiently, all the skin should rub off with no difficulty. Any remaining bits of skin can be easily removed with a sharp knife. This is the Gerry method! Cut the peppers in half and remove the seeds and membrane. Place the peppers in the food processor or liquidizer, add the egg, garlic, parsley and olive oil. Whizz together very thoroughly to make a smooth yellow, green-flecked sauce. Tip the pasta into the boiling water, stir and return to the boil. Cook until tender. Drain and return to the hot pan. Add the sauce and toss everything together thoroughly. Transfer to a warmed platter and serve at once, with freshly grated Parmesan cheese offered separately.

Pasta with a Yellow Pepper Sauce (page 53): the flavour of a roasted pepper makes an unusual sauce.

Pasta with a Spinach Sauce (page 56). A wonderfully creamy spinach option, made without cream.

PASTA WITH A SPINACH SAUCE

Pasta con Salsa di Spinaci

SERVES 6

The delicious flavour of fresh spinach is best for this dish, although frozen can be used in an emergency. The nutmeg gives a special flavour to the dish, and the raw spinach adds crunch.

●

800 g (1¾ lb) fresh spinach
50 g (2 oz) unsalted butter
50 g (2 oz) plain flour
500 ml (17 fl oz) milk
a pinch of freshly grated nutmeg
450 g (1 lb) pasta of your choice
salt and freshly milled black pepper

TO SERVE
freshly grated Parmesan

●

METHOD

Clean and pick over all the spinach and remove the tough stalks. Wash it carefully in several changes of cold water and set aside one large handful. Cram the rest of it into a large pan and cover tightly with a lid. Place over a medium heat and cook until just wilted without adding any liquid. Drain the spinach, reserving the liquid remaining in the pan and then squeeze the wilted leaves dry. Keeping them separate, chop both the raw and cooked spinach finely.

Melt the butter in a pan until foaming, remove from the heat and stir in the flour. When the butter and flour have formed a paste, quickly stir in the milk and whisk energetically to remove any lumps. Add the nutmeg and dilute the sauce further with some of the water from the cooked spinach. You need a fairly thin sauce. Bring a pan of salted water to a rolling boil, including the remaining spinach water. Add the pasta, stir and return to the boil. While the pasta cooks, stir the cooked and raw spinach into the sauce. As soon as the pasta is cooked, drain it thoroughly. Return it to the hot pan, pour over the sauce, toss and tip out on to a warmed platter. Serve with freshly grated Parmesan cheese separately.

PASTA WITH A MEAT AND TOMATO SAUCE

Pasta al Sugo di Carne e Pomodoro

SERVES 6

This is my version of the most simple meat and tomato sauce for pasta. It is absolutely not a Bolognese sauce, which contains about 20 ingredients and requires a long, long cooking time.

•

2 tablespoons olive oil
1 garlic clove, chopped
1 onion, chopped
1 carrot, chopped
1 celery stick, chopped
3 sprigs of fresh parsley, chopped
300 g (11 oz) lean minced beef or veal
4 tablespoons dry red wine
400 g (14 oz) passata
salt and freshly milled black pepper
450 g (1 lb) pasta of your choice

TO SERVE
freshly grated Parmesan

•

METHOD

Fry the olive oil with all the chopped vegetables and the parsley until the onion is soft, stirring frequently. Then add the meat and fry until well browned but not hardened. Stir in the wine and simmer for 2 minutes. Pour in the passata, then stir and season to taste. Cover and simmer for about 1 hour, but the longer the better.

Bring a large pan of salted water to a rolling boil, tip in the pasta and return to the boil. Stir and leave to boil until tender, then drain thoroughly and return to the hot pan. Pour over the hot sauce and toss everything together very thoroughly. Transfer to a warmed serving bowl or platter and serve with freshly grated Parmesan cheese offered separately.

OVERLEAF: Pasta with a Meat and Tomato Sauce, a classic favourite, made the authentic way.

MEAT

· · · · · · · · · · · · ·

The second course, which in traditional Italian cooking and eating habits follows a pasta, soup or risotto course, (il primo) is not always as important as the first course. In fact, in many modern Italian households, families quite often choose to eat either a main course or a first course, rather than eating both. The golden age of four-course lunches followed by four-hour siestas is not quite as popular as it used to be, except, of course, for special occasions like weddings or birthdays.

The meat which is cooked in Italy on a day by day basis tends to be really very lean, as this is what the average housewife likes to feed to her family. Meat is usually cooked in the simplest possible way, allowing the flavour of the meat itself to shine. Very, very rarely are complex sauces permitted to cloud the existing flavour of good quality meat. The contorno, or accompanying vegetables, are also extremely important, although they are usually very simply presented. Here is a selection of various different kinds of meat dishes, which represent some of the most popular recipes cooked in households all over the country almost daily.

ESCALOPES WITH LEMON AND HERBS

Scaloppine al Limone con le Erbette

SERVES 6

A very light, fresh-tasting recipe has just the right level of acidity to freshen the palate. This dish is perfect to follow any pasta or risotto course. Try varying the herbs according to your taste, using more than one if you wish.

●

6 veal or turkey escalopes or small boneless chicken breasts
3 tablespoons plain white flour
I tablespoon olive oil
2 tablespoons chopped fresh parsley
juice and grated zest of I lemon
salt and freshly milled black pepper
2 tablespoons dry white wine

TO SERVE
lemon wedges

●

METHOD

Trim the meat, cut each piece in half and flatten them all evenly with a meat mallet, covering the meat with a sheet of plastic to prevent tearing. Coat the meat lightly in flour and shake off any excess.

Heat the olive oil in a frying pan and seal the meat on one side, turn it over and sprinkle with the parsley, lemon zest and juice. Lower the heat and cook for about 4 minutes, then turn the meat over again. Season to taste with salt and pepper and allow the meat time to cook all the way through, about 5 minutes for thin turkey or chicken, slightly less for veal.

Take the meat out of the pan and arrange on a warmed serving dish. Pour the wine into the pan and scrape the bottom, mixing the contents of the pan with the wine. Tip the juices from the pan over the meat, garnish with the lemon wedges and serve at once.

OVERLEAF: Escalopes with Lemon and Herbs: sizzling hot, deliciously tangy, a classic of Italian cuisine.

SIMPLE STEW

Spezzatino Semplice

SERVES 6

This is a great family favourite. Be sure to give the meat sufficient time to cook so that it becomes really tender and flaky. As with all slow-cooked stews, make sure the meat you start with is of good quality and full of flavour.

●

1.2 kg (2½ lb) boned beef shin
5 tablespoons olive oil
2–3 leaves fresh sage
2–3 sprigs of fresh rosemary
2 tablespoons concentrated tomato purée,
diluted in a tea cup of warm water
about 300 ml (10 fl oz) beef stock
450 g (1 lb) potatoes, cubed
300 g (11 oz) shelled fresh or frozen peas
4 large carrots, cut into large cubes
salt and freshly milled black pepper

●

METHOD

Trim the meat and cut it all into even cubes. Heat the olive oil in a flameproof casserole with the herbs for a few minutes, then add the meat and seal it all over. Lower the heat and pour in the diluted tomato purée. Pour in enough stock just to cover the meat, cover and simmer very gently for about 30–45 minutes, stirring occasionally. Add the potatoes, peas and carrots. Cover and continue to cook for a further 20–30 minutes or until the vegetables are cooked. Taste and season with salt and pepper then transfer to a warmed platter and serve at once.

ESCALOPES WITH WHITE WINE AND ORANGE

Scaloppine al Vino Bianco e Arancio

SERVES 6

As an alternative to the white wine you can also use a dry, white vermouth to make this dish.

•

12 veal or turkey escalopes or 6 small boneless chicken breasts
3 tablespoons plain white flour
2 tablespoons olive oil
150 ml (5 fl oz) dry white wine
salt and freshly milled black pepper
juice and grated zest of $\frac{1}{2}$ orange
1 tablespoon unsalted butter

•

METHOD

Trim all the meat, cut each piece in half and flatten them with a meat mallet, covering the meat with a sheet of plastic to prevent tearing. Coat the meat lightly in the flour, shaking off any excess.

Heat the olive oil in a frying pan and seal the meat quickly in the hot oil on both sides. Pour over the white wine and turn the meat over several times in the wine as it boils off. When the meat is cooked through, season to taste with salt and pepper then take it out of the pan and keep warm.

Add the orange juice and zest to the pan, stir together quickly and then add the butter. Using a balloon whisk, beat the butter into the liquid. Return the meat to the pan, heat through quickly, then transfer meat and sauce on to a warmed platter and serve at once.

Overleaf: Escalopes with White Wine and Orange: melt-in-the-mouth escalopes with a simple, light sauce.

STEWED MINUTE STEAK WITH A GARLIC AND TOMATO SAUCE

Bistecchina all'Aglio e Pomodoro

SERVES 6

This is a version of the classical Pizzaiola dish. Best made with beef or veal, you can use pork or chicken if you prefer. Always serve this dish with lots of crusty bread to mop up the sauce.

•

6 minute steaks or other thin steaks
$\frac{1}{4}$ onion, finely chopped
3 garlic cloves, crushed
3 tablespoons olive oil
a large pinch of dried oregano
200 ml (7 fl oz) passata
salt and freshly milled black pepper
2 tablespoons chopped fresh parsley
1 tablespoon chopped fresh marjoram (optional)

•

METHOD

Trim and prepare the meat first. Use a meat mallet to tenderize the meat as much as possible. Fry the onion and garlic in the olive oil until the onion is very tender. Add the oregano and pour in the passata. Stir and season with salt and pepper. Bring to a simmer and simmer for about 15–20 minutes. Add the meat and simmer for about 10 minutes, or less if you prefer your meat to be quite rare, turning the meat once or twice. Sprinkle with the fresh herbs, and season again with salt and pepper. Transfer to a warmed platter and serve.

LAMB CASSEROLE WITH PEAS

Spezzatino di Agnello con i Piselli

SERVES 6

In southern Italy, lamb is very popular and is cooked in many different and delicious recipes. Here is an unusual dish which makes the most of spring lamb and the sweetness of fresh peas.

•

5 tablespoons olive oil
I large onion, thinly sliced
I kg (2¼ lb) boned shoulder of lamb, trimmed and cubed
100 ml (4 fl oz) dry white wine
800 g (1¾ lb) shelled fresh peas, or frozen peas
6 eggs, beaten
100 g (4 oz) Pecorino, grated
2 tablespoons chopped fresh parsley
salt and freshly milled black pepper

•

METHOD

Fry the olive oil and the onion together until the onion is softened. Add the lamb and seal the meat on all sides, then pour over the wine and boil off the wine for about 1 minute. Season with salt and pepper, cover tightly, lower the heat and simmer for about 20 minutes. Stir in the peas and continue to simmer until the peas and meat are cooked through.

Pre-heat the oven to 200°C/400°F/gas 6. Transfer the meat and peas to an oven-proof dish. Beat the eggs, cheese and parsley together and pour this mixture over the meat and peas. Bake in the pre-heated oven for about 10 minutes or until set and well browned, then serve at once.

Lamb Casserole with Peas (page 69). A comforting and cheap dish, best made with end-of-season peas.

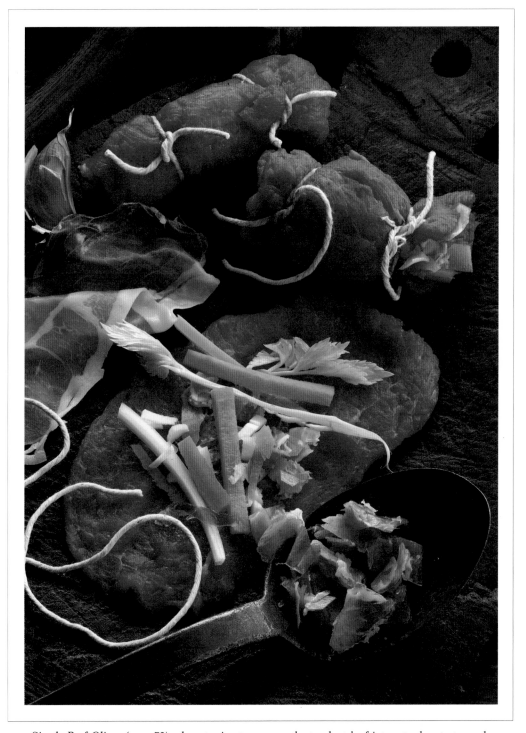

Simple Beef Olives (page 72): slow stewing turns even the toughest beef into a tender, tasty meal.

SIMPLE BEEF OLIVES

Involtini Semplici

SERVES 6

This dish looks as though you've worked so hard to put it together when in fact it is simplicity itself, and a marvellous way to use a cheap cut of meat. It tastes excellent with lemon-flavoured mashed potatoes (just add the juice and grated rind of a lemon) and a green vegetable. If you are not sure of slicing the meat neatly, ask your butcher to do it for you.

•

3 tablespoons olive oil
I onion, chopped
550 g (I lb) fresh ripe tomatoes, skinned, seeded and coarsely chopped
salt and freshly milled black pepper
about I kg (2¼ lb) beef skirt, sliced into 12 little slices weighing about 75 g (3 oz) each
150 g (5 oz) cured ham, coarsely chopped
2 garlic cloves, chopped
3 carrots, cut into 12 batons
3 celery sticks, cut into 12 batons

TO SERVE
lemon-flavoured mashed potatoes

•

METHOD

Heat the olive oil in a wide pan with the onion for a few minutes or until the onion is soft, then add the tomatoes. Season with salt and pepper, cover and leave to simmer gently for about 5 minutes while you prepare the beef olives.

Prepare the meat carefully, putting aside any scraps to use in another recipe. Take each slice of meat and place a little chopped ham, a little chopped garlic and a baton each of carrot and celery in the centre of each one. Roll up the slice of meat around the filling and secure with wooden cocktail sticks or cook's string. Slide the beef olives into the tomato sauce, cover and simmer gently for 40 minutes, turning frequently. Take out of the pan and remove the cocktail sticks or string. Serve at once on a bed of lemony mashed potatoes and drizzle over all the remaining sauce.

LEMON-FLAVOURED MEATBALLS

Polpettine al Limone

SERVES 6

If you happen to be on a self-catering holiday somewhere like Greece or southern Italy, or even Florida, you can improve upon this dish still further by cooking the meatballs in between two leaves from a lemon tree, secured with wooden cocktail sticks so that the meat doesn't fall out during the cooking process. Delicious either on the barbecue or prepared under the grill.

●

750 g ($1\frac{1}{2}$ lb) minced beef or other meat

1 egg

100 g (4 oz) Pecorino or Parmesan, grated

3 garlic cloves, chopped

$\frac{1}{2}$ red onion, finely chopped

3 tablespoons chopped fresh parsley

grated zest of 1 large lemon

juice of $\frac{1}{2}$ lemon

salt and freshly milled black pepper

2 eggs, beaten

5–6 tablespoons dried breadcrumbs

●

METHOD

Mix together the meat, using your hands if possible, with the egg, cheese, garlic, onion and parsley. Add the lemon zest and the juice, then season generously with salt and pepper. Divide the mixture into little balls about the size of an apricot. Flatten them lightly with the palm of your hand, then toss them in the egg and breadcrumbs. Arrange the meatballs on a grill pan or on the barbecue. Grill them for 10–15 minutes, turning frequently, until cooked through then serve them piping hot.

OVERLEAF: Lemon-flavoured Meatballs, a perfect barbecue treat.

MEATBALLS IN PARMA HAM

Polpette con Prosciutto Crudo

SERVES 6

To prevent the cocktail sticks from burning, soak them in cold water for about two hours before using. These little meatballs are excellent to take on a picnic.

●

450 g (1 lb) lean minced beef or veal
grated zest of $\frac{1}{2}$ lemon
2 heaped tablespoons chopped fresh parsley
salt and freshly milled black pepper
2 eggs
2 tablespoons fresh breadcrumbs
6 large slices prosciutto di Parma, halved
2 tablespoons olive oil

●

METHOD

Pre-heat the grill to medium. Mix the minced meat with the zest and parsley. Season with salt and pepper and blend in the eggs. Add sufficient breadcrumbs to make a texture which you can easily shape – not too wet and not too dry. Divide the mixture into 12 small balls and wrap each one in half a slice of prosciutto, securing it with a wooden cocktail stick. Grill the meatballs on all sides, turning frequently and brushing generously and often with olive oil. Serve warm or cold.

POT-ROASTED PORK IN MILK

Maiale al Latte

SERVES 6

This classic dish makes a marvellously warming winter supper dish. The more traditional version calls for the meat to be marinated in wine for two or three days before cooking it slowly in the milk. I think this version is much easier to make, considerably less expensive, and just as delicious. Make sure you cook it over a very gentle heat for the best results.

●

about I kg (2¼ lb) pork joint suitable for pot roasting, such as shoulder
75 g (3 oz) butter
2 onions, thinly sliced
I carrot, thinly sliced
I–2 celery sticks, chopped
2 tablespoons chopped fresh parsley
500 ml (17 fl oz) skimmed or full cream milk
salt and freshly milled black pepper

●

METHOD

If the butcher has not done it for you, tie your joint of pork securely with cook's string so that it holds its shape whilst cooking. Melt the butter and fry all the vegetables and the parsley in a flameproof casserole large enough to take the meat and all the milk. Seal the pork all over in the softened vegetables to brown it thoroughly, then cover and continue to cook the meat slowly over a very low heat, gradually adding the milk as you go along. Season the meat with salt and pepper and turn it frequently in the milk for about 45 minutes. As soon as it is ready, take it out of the casserole and remove the string. Slice the meat and arrange it on a warmed platter. Pour over the sauce which will have formed in the casserole with the milk, the juices from the meat and the vegetables, then serve.

GRILLED STEAKS WITH BALSAMIC VINEGAR

Bistecche alla Griglia con Aceto Balsamico

SERVES 6

This must be one of the simplest and most delicious ways of using balsamic vinegar, the wonderful elixir of the city of Modena, which is now easily available all over the world. Naturally, the steaks are also delicious if cooked on the barbecue.

●

6 sirloin steaks
salt and freshly milled black pepper
3–4 teaspoons balsamic vinegar

●

METHOD

Pre-heat the grill. Trim the steaks and arrange them on the grill. Sprinkle with salt and pepper. Grill them on both sides until they are cooked to the required stage, on each side: blue (1 minute), rare (2 minutes), medium rare (3–4 minutes), medium (4–5 minutes) or well done (7–8 minutes). Transfer them on a warmed platter and sprinkle all over on one side with the balsamic vinegar. Serve at once.

Grilled Steaks with Balsamic Vinegar: it amazes me how the vinegar really lifts the flavour of a steak.

CHICKEN
DISHES

· · · · · · · · · · · · · ·

*Chicken is universally popular and one of the most versatile of ingredients.
It is affordable, lean and tender. I do like to try and buy free-range chickens
whenever possible; it is quite extraordinary how different they taste from poor
old battery-raised birds. In this section I have tried to cover as many different
ways of cooking chicken as I could think of: casseroles, roasts, pan frying,
poaching and grilling. All the recipes which follow are firm favourites, enjoyed
by many families like mine.*

CHICKEN WITH PEPPERS

Pollo ai Peperoni

S E R V E S   6

I really adore this very typical home-cooked dish, it reminds me so much of those endless hot summers in Rome. The sweet, tangy flavour of the peppers is just perfect with the chicken. Frascati is the wine traditionally used in this recipe.

●

2 chickens, about 750 g (1$\frac{1}{2}$ lb) each
4 tablespoons olive oil
3 garlic cloves, thinly sliced
100 ml (4 fl oz) dry white wine
3 juicy, thick peppers, seeded and sliced into strips
450 g (1 lb) fresh ripe tomatoes, skinned, seeded and coarsely chopped
salt and freshly milled black pepper

●

M E T H O D

Clean and trim the chicken, then joint it. Alternatively, buy chicken joints or buy whole chickens and ask your butcher to joint them for you. Heat the olive oil in a wide, deep pan with the garlic for about 5 minutes. Add the chicken joints and brown them all over, sprinkling with the wine. Add the peppers and tomatoes. Season with salt and pepper, cover and simmer for about 40 minutes until cooked through. Serve hot or cold, but not chilled.

OVERLEAF: Chicken with Peppers, simply a slice of authentic Roman cuisine.

DEVILLED CHICKEN

Pollo alla Diavola

SERVES 6 GENEROUSLY

This way of cooking a chicken simply could not be more simple, but the finished result is really delicious. Tastes best of all if eaten with your fingers!

•

2 oven-ready chickens, about 750g (1½ lb) each
about 6 tablespoons olive oil
salt and freshly milled black pepper

•

METHOD

Cut open the chickens along the breast bones to open them out and flatten them as much as possible. You can ask your butcher to do this for you, but it really is very simple and satisfying to do.

Pre-heat the grill. Press the chickens open, pushing hard downwards and outwards to make them as flat as possible. Rub it all over with olive oil, salt and pepper. Grill them on both sides until completely cooked through. You should end up with very well browned, in fact blackened, exteriors and well-cooked but juicy middles. Joint the chickens and serve at once.

CHICKEN CASSEROLE WITH AUBERGINES

Pollo alla Siciliana

SERVES 6

This is just one version of that ubiquitous Italian dish called Cacciatora. Rabbit and chicken are both often called alla Cacciatora. *There is no definitive recipe, as every corner of the country seems to have its own interpretation. One of my favourites is this delicious Sicilian version.*

●

2 aubergines, sliced

salt

3 tablespoons olive oil

2 garlic cloves, crushed

I chicken, about 1.5 kg (3 lb), jointed

5 tablespoons dry white wine

450 g (I lb) ripe tomatoes, skinned, seeded and

coarsely chopped

freshly milled black pepper

2 tablespoons plain white flour

200 ml (7 fl oz) olive oil for frying

●

METHOD

Put the sliced aubergines in a colander and sprinkle them with salt. Put a plate on top and weigh the plate down. Put the colander in the sink and let the aubergines drain for a couple of hours. Meanwhile heat the oil in a large flameproof casserole with the garlic. Brown the chicken joints all over in the oil and garlic, then discard the garlic. Sprinkle the chicken with the wine, then add the tomatoes. Stir everything together thoroughly and season with salt and pepper. Cover and leave to simmer for about 30 minutes or until the chicken is cooked through. Meanwhile, rinse and dry the aubergine slices, then dip them in flour. Heat the frying oil until a little piece of bread dropped into the oil sizzles instantly. Fry the floured aubergine slices on both sides until softened and golden, then drain on kitchen paper. Stir the aubergine slices into the chicken casserole, heat through thoroughly and serve.

Chicken Casserole with Aubergines (page 85). One version of chicken Cacciatora.

Chicken Breasts with a Cheese Filling (page 88): make sure you choose a flavourful cheese.

CHICKEN BREASTS WITH A CHEESE FILLING

Petti di Pollo con Ripieno di Formaggio

SERVES 6

I like to vary this dish with different kinds of cheese such as Gorgonzola, Groviera or Mozzarella, depending upon how strongly flavoured I like it to be. I find that most children tend not to be so keen on blue cheese, so when I prepare it for them I tend to stick to blander cheeses like Fontina or Emmenthal. Sometimes I make a simple tomato sauce to go with it, which I either serve separately in a sauce boat or pour over the finished dish just before serving.

•

4 plump chicken breasts, skinned and boned
350 g (12 oz) Fontina or Emmenthal, sliced into strips
4 tablespoons olive oil
2 leaves fresh sage or $\frac{1}{2}$ teaspoon rubbed sage leaves
salt and freshly milled black pepper

•

METHOD

Trim the chicken breasts and make a long incision down the side of each one to create a pocket. Slip a few slices of the cheese inside each chicken breast and close the incision securely with cocktail sticks.

Heat the olive oil in a wide frying pan with the sage for about 5 minutes, then lay the chicken in the hot flavoured oil and seal on both sides. When the chicken is golden brown, sprinkle with the salt and pepper and turn the heat down low. Cover and simmer very gently for about 10–15 minutes or until the chicken is cooked through and the cheese has melted. Transfer to a warmed platter, remove the cocktail sticks and serve.

ITALIAN ROAST CHICKEN

Pollo Arrosto all'Italiana

SERVES 6

The flavour of chicken roasted in this way varies according to the herbs you want to add to the mixture. You can make it more or less pungent as you prefer, or according to what you serve alongside it. I always serve potatoes, crisply roasted in olive oil and garlic.

•

5 tablespoons olive oil
3 tablespoons fresh rosemary or sage leaves, or fresh marjoram
or a combination of all three, finely chopped
4 garlic cloves, finely chopped
I large chicken, about 1.5 kg (3 lb), jointed
salt and freshly milled black pepper
water or chicken stock for basting

•

METHOD

Pre-heat the oven to 200°C/400°F/gas 6. Put the olive oil in a roasting tin and add the herbs and garlic. Add the chicken and mix it thoroughly with the oil, turning the joints over to coat them thoroughly. Sprinkle generously with salt and pepper, then place in the oven to roast for about 40 minutes until cooked through, crisp and golden brown, turning the joints over and basting occasionally with a little water or chicken stock. Serve hot or cold.

OVERLEAF: Italian Roast Chicken, glowing golden chicken joints packed with flavour.

CHICKEN CASSEROLE WITH TOMATO AND ROSEMARY

Pollo al Rosmarino e Pomodoro

SERVES 6

Rosemary is a herb which matches the flavour of chicken perfectly. In this recipe there is always plenty of sauce left to mop up with some crusty Italian bread.

•

6 chicken breasts, boned and skinned
6 tablespoons olive oil
3 garlic cloves, finely chopped
3 teaspoons fresh rosemary leaves or 1½ teaspoons dried rosemary
450 ml (15 fl oz) passata or canned chopped tomatoes
salt and freshly milled black pepper

TO SERVE
crusty Italian bread

•

METHOD

Trim the chicken carefully. Heat the olive oil in a frying pan with the garlic and rosemary. Fry for about 4 minutes, then lay the chicken in the oil and brown it on both sides.

When the chicken is browned and sealed on both sides, pour over the passata. Season with salt and pepper. Cover and simmer gently for about 15 minutes or until the chicken is cooked through. Transfer to a warmed platter and serve immediately with crusty bread.

POACHED CHICKEN

Pollo Lesso

SERVES 6

When I was a child, this was one of my favourite things to eat. In those days, it was easy to buy boiling fowls, which tended to have more flavour than a neat, oven-ready bird. They are somewhat less easily available these days, but you can find them if you look hard enough.

•

1 oven-ready chicken or boiling fowl, about 1.5 kg (3 lb)
2 celery sticks with leaves, quartered
2 carrots, quartered
1 onion, halved
salt

•

METHOD

Clean the chicken thoroughly, then lay it in a large pan. Just cover with water, add the vegetables and a little salt. Cover and boil gently for about $1\frac{1}{2}$ hours or until the chicken is cooked through.

Remove the chicken from the pan and drain it (reserving the stock for another dish). Joint and slice it into sections. Serve warm with a sharp mayonnaise (normal mayonnaise seasoned with extra lemon juice or white wine vinegar).

LEMON AND TARRAGON CHICKEN

Pollo al Limone e Dragoncello

SERVES 6

If you want to vary the flavour of this dish a little, you can use half orange juice and half lemon juice. The fresh tarragon added at the end just finishes it off perfectly.

●

25 g (1 oz) unsalted butter
3 tablespoons olive oil
6 chicken joints
salt and freshly milled black pepper
250 ml (8 fl oz) chicken stock
3 egg yolks
juice and grated zest of 1 lemon
about 10 leaves fresh tarragon, chopped

●

METHOD

Heat the butter and olive oil together in a deep pan, then seal the chicken joints quickly in the hot fat. Sprinkle with salt and pepper, then cover with the stock. Turn the heat down, cover with a lid and simmer gently for about 45 minutes until the chicken is cooked through.

Take the chicken out of the pan and arrange on a warmed platter. Raise the heat under the pan and beat the egg yolks and lemon juice and zest into the juices remaining in the pan with a balloon whisk. Pour this over the cooked chicken and sprinkle with the fresh tarragon. Serve at once.

Lemon and Tarragon Chicken: an elegant dish of Tuscan origin.

GREEN BEAN AND CHICKEN SALAD

Insalata di Pollo e Fagiolini

SERVES 6

This is a very quick dish which somehow manages to impress. The most important thing is to arrange the salad in a really pretty bowl and to serve it quickly before the salad leaves begin to wilt dramatically.

•

3 little gem lettuces, broken into leaves
1 oak leaf lettuce, broken into leaves and torn into bite-sized pieces
1 head radicchio, torn into bite-sized pieces
salt
225 g (8 oz) fine green beans, topped and tailed
3 tablespoons olive oil
1 garlic clove, crushed
3 chicken breasts, cut into finger-sized strips

FOR THE DRESSING
2 tablespoons white wine vinegar
$\frac{1}{4}$ teaspoon salt
$\frac{1}{2}$ teaspoon mustard of your choice
6 twists of freshly milled black pepper
175 ml (6 fl oz) extra virgin olive oil

•

METHOD

Wash and dry all the salad leaves thoroughly, then arrange them all in a wide salad bowl. Bring a pan of salted water to the boil and cook the beans for a few minutes until just tender. Meanwhile, heat the olive oil with the crushed garlic, then quickly stir-fry all the chicken strips until crisp and cooked through.

Put all the dressing ingredients in a screw-top jar and screw on the lid tightly. Shake the dressing until well mixed and thickened. Drain the hot beans and tip them over the salad leaves. Scatter the cooked, hot chicken over the beans and salad leaves. Sprinkle with the dressing and serve at once.

CHICKEN SALTIMBOCCA

Saltimbocca di Pollo

SERVES 6

This is the chicken version of the classic veal dish. The tang of the sage really comes through and makes for a very special flavour.

●

3 large chicken breasts
6 slices Mozzarella
12 leaves fresh sage
3 slices prosciutto crudo (cured ham), halved
5 tablespoons olive oil
3 tablespoons dry white wine
salt and freshly milled black pepper

●

METHOD

Cut the chicken breasts in half so that you end up with 6 slices of thickish chicken breast. Trim and tidy them as much as possible. Lay a slice of Mozzarella on top of each chicken breast, lay two sage leaves on top of each slice of cheese and cover each one with a slice of *prosciutto*. Use wooden cocktail sticks to secure everything in place during the cooking process. Heat the olive oil in a wide frying pan, then lay the chicken breasts in the hot oil side by side. Cook on one side for about 5–6 minutes, then turn them over. Pour over the wine and season with salt and pepper. Finish cooking on the other side for a further 5–6 minutes then transfer to a warmed serving dish.

Remove the cocktail sticks. Pour any remaining juices from the pan over the cooked chicken and serve at once.

OVERLEAF: Chicken Saltimbocca, the secret is in the thin sheets of proscuitto crudo.

FISH DISHES

. . . .

I don't know if the same is true in other parts of the world, but Italians tend to order fish at the restaurant much more often than they cook it at home. I think this shows a basic insecurity about cooking fish, maybe because of the cooking smell which appears to put a lot of people off, or a mistaken idea that cooking fish is somehow much more difficult than cooking meat or chicken. In fact, cooking fish can be incredibly easy, it does not have to make your entire house smell for days on end, and most important of all, fish, especially oily fish, is really very good for you. This selection of recipes could not be easier to prepare, and all rely on everyday ingredients. Now that fresh fish is so much more readily available and the range we can buy has widened so enormously, it is time to start enjoying fish at home much more often.

MACKEREL WITH WHITE WINE AND TOMATOES

Sgombri al Vino Bianco e Pomodoro

SERVES 6

The humble mackerel is an extremely delicious and sadly underrated fish. In this recipe, it is baked with garlic, white wine and tomatoes to make a lovely main course dish. Serve with boiled potatoes and green salad.

●

6 large or 12 smaller mackerel, heads and all bones removed
3 tablespoons plain white flour
6 tablespoons olive oil
salt and freshly milled black pepper
4 garlic cloves, finely chopped
200 ml (7 fl oz) dry white wine
6 ripe tomatoes, sliced

●

METHOD

Pre-heat the oven to 190°C/375°F/gas 5. Wash and dry the mackerel carefully, then coat lightly on both sides with the flour. Oil an ovenproof dish and arrange the mackerel in the dish side by side. Sprinkle with a little more oil, salt and pepper and the garlic. Bake in the pre-heated oven for 15 minutes, then begin to baste with the wine, adding it gradually every 5–6 minutes.

Within about 15 minutes, the fish should be cooked through. Cover it with the tomato slices and sprinkle the remaining oil over the top. Increase the oven temperature to 220°C/425°F/gas 7. Bake for a further 5 minutes then serve.

MACKEREL AND PEAS

Sgombri con Piselli

SERVES 6

Another delicious recipe for the much underrated mackerel, though you could use another kind of fish if you prefer.

●

6 large or 12 smaller mackerel, heads and all bones removed
6 tablespoons olive oil
1 onion, chopped
salt
2 tablespoons chopped fresh parsley
450 g (1 lb) fresh shelled peas or frozen peas
3 tablespoons tomato purée diluted in a tea cup of hot water

●

METHOD

Trim and wash the fish, pat dry and set to one side until required. Fry the olive oil and onion together until the onion is transparent. Add the fish and fry until just coloured on both sides. Sprinkle with salt and then scatter over the parsley. Add the peas and the diluted tomato purée. Cover and simmer for about 10–15 minutes until the peas are tender. Transfer on to a warmed platter and serve at once.

Mackerel and Peas: you can cook the mackerel whole or in fillets, the choice is yours.

GRILLED FISH

Pesce alla Griglia

SERVES 6

One of the oldest and most perfect ways to cook fish so that it retains all its natural goodness and flavour. If you can barbecue it over a wood fire, you will turn a basically wonderful meal into something very special. I have suggested a grey mullet, but any solid, firm, whole fish will work equally well.

●

I large grey mullet, weighing about 1.5 kg (3 lb), gutted and scaled
salt and freshly milled black pepper
8 small sprigs fresh thyme
4 tablespoons olive oil
best quality olive oil and lemon wedges to serve

●

METHOD

Pre-heat the grill, or light the barbecue. Wash and dry the fish carefully. Make 4 slits through the skin on either side of the fish. Place the point of the knife through the open belly of the gutted fish and loosen the flesh away from both sides of the back bone slightly to help the fish cook through. Sprinkle with salt and pepper inside and out, and insert the thyme into the incisions you have made on the sides.

Place the fish under the grill and cook for about 10 minutes on each side, brushing occasionally with the olive oil as the fish cooks. When the fish is cooked through, it will be well browned on the outside and soft, moist and flaky on the inside. Serve with a little very good quality olive oil to drizzle over each portion and lemon wedges so everybody can squeeze a little lemon juice over their portion if they wish.

BAKED FISH ON A BED OF ROSEMARY, POTATOES AND GARLIC

Pesce Arrosto

SERVES 6

I really love this way of cooking fish. I can never decide which is more delicious, the potatoes or the fish itself! A bream, bass, grey mullet or other whole, solid fish is best, but any other kind of fish, filleted or whole, will also work quite well.

●

I whole fish such as a grey mullet or a bream,
about 1.5 kg (3 lb), gutted and scaled
6 potatoes, sliced to 1 cm ($\frac{1}{2}$ in) thickness
8 tablespoons olive oil
salt and freshly milled black pepper
4 garlic cloves, unpeeled and crushed
4 sprigs of fresh rosemary

●

METHOD

Pre-heat the oven to gas mark 190°C/375°F/gas 5. Wash and dry the fish thoroughly inside and out. Put all the potato slices in an ovenproof dish and pour about 6 tablespoons of the olive oil over them. Sprinkle generously with salt and pepper and then add the garlic and rosemary. Toss the potatoes with the other ingredients to coat them thoroughly in the olive oil and to distribute the flavour of the garlic and rosemary evenly.

Rub the remaining olive oil all over the fish, both inside and out. Season the fish with salt and pepper inside and out, then lay the fish on top of the potatoes. Bake in the pre-heated oven for 30–40 minutes until the potatoes and the fish are cooked through. If necessary, baste the fish with a little water during the cooking process. Transfer the fish on to a warmed flat platter and arrange the potatoes in a warmed bowl, then serve at once.

OVERLEAF: Baked Fish on a Bed of Rosemary, Potatoes and Garlic, another family classic, often made with fish I catch myself. (But not this time!)

COD FILLETS WITH LEMON JUICE AND WHITE WINE

Filetti di Merluzzo al Vino Bianco e Limone

SERVES 6

This is a very simple and easy way to cook fresh cod fillets. Even frozen cod fillets will be much enhanced by this recipe.

●

12 small cod fillets (enough for 6 people)
2 tablespoons plain flour
3 tablespoons unsalted butter
salt and freshly milled black pepper
juice of $\frac{1}{2}$ lemon
4 tablespoons dry white wine

TO SERVE
lemon wedges

●

METHOD

Rinse and dry the fish fillets thoroughly. Coat the fish in flour. Melt the butter in a wide frying pan and fry the fish on both sides for about 4 minutes. Carefully remove from the pan and put the fillets to one side between two warm plates until required.

Pour the lemon juice and wine into the pan. Stir thoroughly, scraping the pan. Boil the mixture quickly for about 4 minutes, stirring constantly. Slide the fish back into the pan, and heat through for about 3 minutes, spooning the sauce over the fish frequently. Transfer on to a warmed platter, garnish with the lemon wedges and serve at once.

FISH FILLETS IN A TOMATO AND OLIVE SAUCE

Filetti di Pesce al Pomodoro e Olive

SERVES 6

This is a recipe which is guaranteed to make even the dullest cod fillet taste more exciting. Quick and very simple to prepare, ideal with a green salad and some pan-fried potatoes.

●

2 garlic cloves, chopped
4 tablespoons olive oil
250 ml (8 fl oz) passata
$\frac{1}{2}$ teaspoon dried oregano
salt and freshly milled black pepper
12 black olives, stoned and coarsely chopped
12 plaice, sole or small cod fillets

●

METHOD

Fry the garlic gently in a wide frying pan with the olive oil for about 5 minutes, then pour in the passata. Stir and simmer for about 5 minutes, then add the oregano and season with salt and pepper. Stir in the black olives and simmer, covered, for about 15 minutes. Slide in the fish and simmer for about 8 minutes or until cooked through. Remove the fish carefully from the pan and arrange on a warmed platter. Cover with the sauce and serve at once.

Fish Fillets in a Tomato and Olive Sauce (page 109): a dish with lots of contrasting colours.

Prawns in a Tomato Sauce (page 112). Juicy, fat prawns need only simple cooking.

PRAWNS IN A TOMATO SAUCE

Gamberi al Pomodoro

SERVES 6

This is a delectably messy dish, which requires everyone to use their fingers as much as possible in order to really enjoy the prawns. Fingerbowls and napkins are a real must! I realize that in some parts of the world prawns are not the cheapest fish to buy, so remember to make the most of this recipe whenever you are on a self-catering holiday in those parts of the world where prawns are plentiful and very inexpensive!

•

I kg (2¼ lb) fresh raw shell-on large prawns
5 tablespoons olive oil
3 garlic cloves, chopped
250 ml (8 fl oz) passata
salt and freshly milled black pepper
10 leaves fresh basil, torn into small pieces

•

METHOD

Give the prawns a quick rinse in cold fresh water and then pat them dry. Heat the olive oil in a large deep frying pan with the garlic. Fry for about 5 minutes, then add the passata and stir. Cover and simmer for about 5 minutes, then add the prawns and sprinkle generously with salt and pepper. Stir constantly, and cook the prawns over a high heat for about 8 minutes. Cover with a lid and take off the heat. Leave to stand for about 3 minutes, then tip out on to a warmed platter, sprinkle with the basil and serve at once.

RED MULLET WITH CURED HAM

Triglie alla Marchigiana

SERVES 6

In this classical recipe, the red mullet are surrounded by slices of prosciutto crudo *(cured ham)*
and then baked in the oven. The combination of flavours is really marvellous and the dish is
simplicity itself to put together. Small red snapper can be used instead of red mullet.

●

6 plump red mullet
8 tablespoons olive oil
juice of 1 lemon
6 slices proscuitto crudo (cured ham)
4 tablespoons very fine dry breadcrumbs
12 leaves fresh sage
salt and freshly milled black pepper

●

METHOD

Scale and gut the red mullet. Wash them very thoroughly both inside and out and
pat dry. Slit the skin on either side in three or four places. Mix 6 tablespoons of olive
oil with the lemon juice and lay the mullet in this marinade. Leave to stand for about
15 minutes.

Meanwhile, pre-heat the oven to 375°F/190°C/gas mark 5. Grease a baking dish
with the remaining oil. Lay the ham slices on the bottom of the baking dish. Take
the red mullet out of the marinade and roll them in the breadcrumbs, then lay them
on top of the ham, wrap them in the ham, then pack them tightly into the dish. Slip
the sage leaves in between the fish. Pour the marinade all over the fish, season with
salt and pepper and place the dish in the oven. Bake for about 25 minutes or until
the fish are cooked through, basting occasionally with a little water. Transfer the red
mullet and the ham to a warmed dish, and serve.

OVERLEAF: Red Mullet with Cured Ham, the ham and fish look and taste delicious together.

POACHED TROUT

Trota Lessa

SERVES 6

The important thing to remember when poaching fish is to prepare the water in which the fish will cook. This is something which takes virtually no time or effort at all, but makes all the difference to the finished flavour of the dish.

●

1 carrot, scraped and quartered
1 small onion or leek, cleaned and quartered
1 celery stick, washed and quartered
5 sprigs of fresh parsley
$\frac{1}{2}$ lemon
salt
6 black peppercorns
6 small whole trout, about 225 g (8 oz) each

TO SERVE
hollandaise sauce, mayonnaise or olive oil and lemon juice

●

METHOD

Put all the vegetables in a fish kettle or a large pan. Cover generously with cold water. Add the lemon, 2 pinches of salt and the peppercorns. Bring to the boil slowly, covered, and simmer for about 20 minutes. Clean, gut and scale the trout. Wash them all thoroughly under running fresh water, then slip them into the water. Simmer slowly for about 10 minutes, then turn off the heat. Leave the fish in the fish kettle or pan, covered with the lid, until the water is tepid. Remove the fish carefully from the water, drain them and arrange on a dish. Serve warm or cold with hollandaise sauce, mayonnaise or olive oil and lemon juice.

SIMPLE FISH CASSEROLE

Zuppetta di Pesce

S E R V E S   6

This is the easiest recipe for making a really Italian tasting fish casserole. You can add mussels or prawns if you wish, although the basic recipe as it appears below calls only for filleted white fish. The bread soaks up all the flavours and juices of the fish and is eaten at the end, once all the fish has been enjoyed.

●

1.5 kg (3 lb) approximately filleted fish of various kinds:
cod, monkfish, haddock, plaice etc.
8 tablespoons olive oil
4 garlic cloves, finely chopped
4 tablespoons chopped fresh parsley
salt and freshly milled black pepper
about 200 ml (7 fl oz) fish stock
1 garlic clove, left whole
12 thin slices ciabatta bread, toasted

●

M E T H O D

Prepare all the fish first. Trim it carefully, then wash and dry it all. Heat the olive oil in a deep pan with the garlic and the parsley for about 5 minutes. Add all the fish and stir. Season with salt and pepper and pour over the fish stock. Cover tightly and simmer very gently for about 15 minutes. Rub the toasted bread with the garlic and use the bread to line a large, wide-brimmed and warmed bowl. Pour the hot fish casserole over the bread and serve at once.

OVERLEAF: Simple Fish Casserole, the freshest fish available and a varied selection will guarantee the success of this dish.

EGG DISHES

· · · · · · · · · · · · · ·

*These dishes represent an alternative to a meat or fish main course.
They are ideal to serve after an especially filling first course of pasta, or for
people who don't eat meat or fish but still want to enjoy delicious Italian
food. All these recipes are distinctly Italian and very simple to make
with easily available ingredients.*

*It goes without saying that the prerequisite for any successful dish with eggs
is the freshness of the egg. To check if an egg is as fresh as the packaging
or the vendor claims it to be, try this simple old fashioned test. Place an egg
into a bowl containing enough slightly salted cold water to submerge it.
If the egg stays horizontal, it is fresh. If it turns vertical, then the egg
has lost its freshness.*

*Using eggs or cheese either together or separately, is in most people's
estimation perfectly fine for everyday family eating. Most of us find
it quite hard to conceive of serving eggs for a more important occasion, such
as a dinner party. Bearing that in mind, and considering that not all our
dinner party guests are happy eating either meat or fish, amongst the
following ten recipes I have inserted one or two rather more elegant
dishes that you might like to consider for just such events.*

SALAME OMELETTE

Frittata al Salame

SERVES 4

Salame is a cured pork sausage and comes in many different varieties. There are spicy, chilli-coloured salami (salami is the plural of salame!), more bland and sweet versions like Salame Milano, fennel-flavoured salame like finocchiona and very fine, thin salame like felino. Whichever one you choose, it will make a marvellous flavour combination in this flat Italian omelette which can be served either hot or cold.

●

100 g (4 oz) salame of your choice, sliced and cubed
5 eggs
salt and freshly milled black pepper
4 tablespoons freshly grated Parmesan

●

METHOD

Fry the salame gently on its own in a wide, shallow frying pan. (A non-stick pan, or well used omelette pan is necessary in this case.) Beat the eggs in a bowl with a pinch each of salt and pepper and the grated Parmesan. Pour the eggs over the salame and shake the pan to flatten it. Turn the frittata over as soon as it has set and one side is golden brown. Turn it upside down on to a large, flat lid or plate, then slide it back into the pan on the other side. Cook on the underside for a further 4 minutes, then slide on to a warmed platter and serve either hot or cold.

OVERLEAF: Salame Omelette, a really punchy, full-of-flavour salame is what you need for this omelette to be memorable.

POTATO AND CHICKEN LIVER OMELETTE

Frittata di Fegatini e Patate

SERVES 6

*Although chicken livers are not to everyone's taste, you may be converted if you try this frittata
– it makes a perfect brunch served with crusty bread and a tomato salad.*

•

2 fist-sized potatoes, peeled
6 eggs, beaten
salt and freshly milled black pepper
5 chicken livers, trimmed, washed and dried
2 rashers bacon, rinded and diced
4 tablespoons olive oil
2 tablespoons chopped fresh parsley

•

METHOD

Boil the potatoes until tender then drain and dice. Beat and season the eggs. Coarsely
chop the livers and mix with the bacon. Heat half the oil and quickly fry the chick-
en livers and bacon until soft, then remove from the pan and leave to cool. Mix the
eggs and livers and bacon together thoroughly, add the potatoes then stir in the parsley. Heat the remaining oil in a wide, non-stick frying pan. Pour in the egg mixture
and shake the pan. Allow the eggs to set but shake the pan to keep it well loosened.
When the frittata is well browned and set underneath, slide it on to a plate then turn
it back into the hot frying pan the other way up. Allow it to brown on the other side
then transfer to a warmed serving dish.

MINI OMELETTES WITH TOMATO SAUCE

Frittatine al Pomodoro

SERVES 6

Served with a mixed salad and lots of warm, crusty bread, this dish makes a complete meal.

●

8 eggs, beaten
salt and freshly milled black pepper
3 tablespoons unsalted butter or olive oil
150 g (5 oz) Parmesan, freshly grated, or Gruyère, sliced into thin sticks,
or Mozzarella, cubed
2 garlic cloves, finely chopped
$\frac{1}{2}$ onion, finely chopped
3 tablespoons olive oil
300 ml (10 fl oz) passata
2 tablespoons chopped fresh parsley

●

METHOD

Whisk the beaten eggs with salt and pepper. Heat $\frac{1}{2}$ tablespoon of the butter or olive oil in a 15 cm (6 in) frying pan until sizzling, then pour in about one-sixth of the beaten egg or enough to make a thin flat omelette. Let it set on one side then flip over by turning it upside down on a plate or a lid, then slipping it back into the frying pan on the other side. Cook each omelette for 2 minutes on each side, then slide out on to a board or plate. Do the same with all the egg mixture until you have 6 small, cooked omelettes. Divide the cheese among the six omelettes and roll them up around the cheese. Lay the rolled up omelettes with their cheese filling in an oven-proof dish. Pre-heat the oven to 200°C/400°G/gas 6.

Fry the garlic and onion in the olive oil until the onion is transparent. Pour in the passata and season with salt and pepper. Stir in the parsley and cover. Leave to simmer for about 15 minutes, then pour this sauce over the omelettes. Place the dish in the oven to bake for about 10 minutes or until bubbling hot. Serve at once, with a mixed salad and warm, crusty bread to mop up the sauce.

OVERLEAF: Mini Omelettes with Tomato Sauce, best made with the very freshest Mozzarella

HARD-BOILED EGGS STUFFED WITH TUNA

Uova Sode Ripiene al Tonno

SERVES 6

This is a family favourite for picnics. They are also very good for an easy lunch, especially if you arrange the stuffed eggs on a bed of dressed salad leaves. Italian canned tuna in olive oil has by far the best flavour, but if you are watching the calories you can use canned tuna in brine. The capers and gherkins add a note of sharp crunchiness, but leave them out if they are not to your liking.

●

12 eggs, hard-boiled and shelled
150 g (5 oz) canned tuna in olive oil
6 tablespoons mayonnaise
4 teaspoons lemon juice
about 12 capers, rinsed and chopped (optional)
5 pickled gherkins, chopped (optional)
salt and freshly milled black pepper

TO SERVE
salad leaves

●

METHOD

Halve the eggs and remove the yolks. Mash the yolks with a fork. Drain and flake the tuna, then mash it into the egg yolks with the mayonnaise. Mix in the lemon juice, then stir in the capers and the gherkins, if using. Season with salt and pepper. Pile this mixture back into the halved eggs and arrange them on a dish. Garnish with salad leaves and chill until required.

BAKED EGGS WITH PRAWNS

Uova Ripiene di Gamberetti al Forno

SERVES 6

When I was a child, my mother used to make this dish as a family supper about twice a month. Sometimes she would vary the flavour slightly by changing to white flaked fish instead of the prawns. I always did, and still do, prefer the prawn version!

●

6 eggs, hard-boiled and shelled
225 g (8 oz) shelled cooked prawns
50 g (2 oz) unsalted butter
50 g (2 oz) plain white flour
450 ml (15 fl oz) milk
$\frac{1}{2}$ teaspoon concentrated tomato purée
salt and freshly milled black pepper

●

METHOD

Pre-heat the oven to 200°C/400°F/gas 6. Halve the eggs and remove the yolks. Mash the yolks with a fork, then add the prawns to the yolks. Melt the butter in a pan until foaming, stir in the flour and heat until it forms a paste that comes away from the sides of the pan. Pour in the milk and whisk energetically until smooth. Stir in the tomato purée and season with salt and pepper. Boil gently until thickened, and until the flavour of raw flour has disappeared completely. Cool. Pour about half of the cooled sauce over the yolks and prawn mixture. Mix together and then fill the halved eggs generously. Place the filled eggs in an ovenproof dish, pour over the remaining sauce and place in the oven to bake for about 10 minutes until just browned and bubbling hot. Serve at once.

OVERLEAF: Baked Eggs with Prawns, a very special family favourite.

SPINACH OMELETTE

Frittata di Spinaci

SERVES 4–6

This dish is best if made with fresh young spinach, but it is also very good when made with frozen spinach. An alternative is to use fresh Swiss chard which should be cooked in the same way as the fresh spinach.

●

1.75 kg (4 lb) spinach leaves, cooked and carefully drained
6 eggs, beaten
1–2 onions, finely chopped
150 g (5 oz) Parmesan, freshly grated
salt and freshly milled black pepper
4 tablespoons olive oil

●

METHOD

Squeeze the spinach dry in your hands, then chop finely. Mix it into the beaten eggs, then add the onions, Parmesan, salt and pepper.

Heat the olive oil in a wide, shallow pan and when it is very hot, pour in the egg mixture. Shake the pan to flatten and even out the mixture and cook until the underside is browned and firm. Flip the omelette over by turning it upside down on to a flat lid or a plate, then sliding it back into the pan on the other side. Cook until brown and firm on the under side. Slide on to a warmed platter. Serve hot or cold.

EGGS IN TOMATOES

Uova al Pomodoro

SERVES 6

This is probably one of the most interesting ways of serving scrambled eggs. You can make the dish even more interesting by adding a simple tomato sauce or by adding more grated or cubed cheese to the eggs. Beefsteak tomatoes are the best ones to use.

●

6 large ripe tomatoes
6 eggs, beaten
2 tablespoons milk
2 tablespoons freshly grated Parmesan
salt and freshly milled black pepper
butter for greasing

●

METHOD

Pre-heat the oven to 190°C/375°F/gas 5. Slice the tops off the tomatoes and scoop out the seeds. Turn them upside down and let them drain for about 30 minutes. Meanwhile beat the eggs with the milk, Parmesan and salt and pepper. Grease a baking dish thoroughly with butter. Pour the egg mixture into the tomatoes and replace the tops. Arrange the filled tomatoes in the baking dish then place the dish in a roasting tin. Pour enough water into the roasting tin to come about half-way up the sides of the baking dish. Bake in the oven for about 20 minutes or until the eggs have just set and the tomatoes are softened but not mushy. Serve immediately.

OVERLEAF: Eggs in Tomatoes, choose ripe, slightly wrinkled, big, juicy tomatoes for this dish.

SALADS

· · · · · · · · · · · · · ·

When I was a child, salad appeared at the table for every single meal, alongside the main course or to accompany a cheese platter. It was a huge, beautiful bowl of fresh, green crisp leaves, sometimes with thinly sliced red onion sprinkled through it, but always dressed with the most fragrant, green and delicious olive oil, a dash of vinegar and a sprinkling of sea salt. My brothers and I all grew up with a tremendous passion for this sort of salad, especially my eldest brother who can single-handedly consume a bowl big enough to wash a baby in filled to the brim! Out of habit, I still always make a green salad with the same kind of dressing for my own family, but it seems to be only me who eats it with the same kind of wild abandon. Perhaps my sons will grow into it, or perhaps the salad has not quite the same, freshness, flavour and sweetness of my own childhood.

My favourite salad above all others is the salad which my mother used to make for me sometimes when I came in from school. It consisted of a bowl of sliced, very fresh, firm, juicy tomatoes, sprinkled generously with dried oregano, doused with olive oil and sprinkled with salt. It was left to stand for about ten minutes while the tomatoes began to exude their juices. When I came to eat it, my chin became shiny with the oil and I needed lots of bread to mop up all the juices. It was, and still is, the best possible afternoon snack, and one which made coming home from school even more memorable.

This chapter includes a selection of salads which are rather more substantial in some cases than the two mentioned above. I have included them particularly with the thought of enjoyment on long, hot summer days.

TUNA AND BEAN SALAD

Insalata di Tonno e Fagioli

SERVES 6

This classic salad makes a marvellously easy starter or even a main course. You can omit the onions if you like, although they really do add a lot of punch to the finished dish. If you can find fresh borlotti beans, they will be much nicer than the canned or dried varieties.

●

300 g (11 oz) canned, fresh or dried cooked borlotti beans
300 g (11 oz) canned tuna in olive oil, flaked
1 large red onion, thinly sliced
2 tablespoons chopped fresh flatleaf parsley
5 tablespoons olive oil
1 tablespoon white wine vinegar
salt and freshly milled black pepper

TO SERVE
crusty bread

●

METHOD

If you are using dried beans, soak them overnight in cold fresh water, then drain and place them in a pan with fresh water. Boil them quickly for 5 minutes. Drain and rinse, then boil slowly in fresh water until tender. Do not add salt to the water until the beans are tender otherwise the skins will toughen. Fresh borlotti beans are cooked in exactly the same way.

Drain the canned or cooked beans carefully and rinse them in cold water. When they are cool, mix them with the flaked tuna. Add the onions and parsley and mix together, then dress with the olive oil, vinegar and salt and pepper. Let the dressed salad stand for about 30 minutes, then serve with plenty of crusty bread to mop up the juices.

Tuna and Bean Salad (page 137). The sweet red onion really lifts the flavour of this salad.

Salad of Mozzarella, Tomatoes and Basil (page 140). A marvellous and classic Italian salad.

SALAD OF MOZZARELLA, TOMATOES AND BASIL

Insalata Tricolore

SERVES 6

No Italian salad collection could possibly be complete without this most traditional and classic recipe. For a really special salad, make sure the Mozzarella is made from buffalo milk (Mozzarella di bufala) and is as fresh as possible. Remember that basil should never be chopped as the leaves bruise so easily, but should ideally be torn into the required size with your fingers.

●

4 large ripe tomatoes, sliced
200 g (7 oz) fresh Mozzarella, sliced
about 12 leaves fresh basil, torn into pieces
8 tablespoons olive oil
salt and freshly milled black pepper

●

METHOD

Arrange the sliced tomatoes on a platter. Lay the Mozzarella slices on top and sprinkle with the basil. Drizzle over the olive oil and finish off with a sprinkling of salt and pepper. Serve at once.

GRILLED VEGETABLE SALAD

Insalata di Verdure alla Griglia

SERVES 6

Grilled vegetables became very trendy and fashionable about five or six years ago. In this salad, all the flavours of the individual vegetables really stand out. Everything always tastes best when grilled over a wood fire, but even when cooked under an ordinary grill these vegetables really are delicious.

●

I aubergine, sliced lengthways

2 courgettes, thinly sliced lengthways

2 peppers, seeded and sliced lengthways

I large onion, sliced across the centre into 8 flat, thick slices

I bulb fennel, sliced into 8 flat, thick slices

4 tomatoes, sliced very thickly across

200 ml (7 fl oz) olive oil

2 garlic cloves, finely chopped

2 tablespoons chopped fresh flatleaf parsley

salt and freshly milled black pepper

I tablespoon red wine vinegar

●

METHOD

Lay the aubergine slices in a colander and sprinkle with salt. Cover with a plate, weigh down and leave to drain for 1 hour, then rinse and pat dry. Heat the grill to medium. Brush the vegetables with some of the olive oil and grill each vegetable in batches until just tender, brushing with more olive oil as they cook. As soon as the vegetables are cooked, arrange them in a shallow, wide bowl and sprinkle with chopped garlic and parsley, then season with salt and pepper. When all the vegetables are grilled and in the bowl, sprinkle the salad with the vinegar and the remaining olive oil. Mix it all together gently, and serve at once.

Grilled Vegetable Salad (page 141). And now for something really colourful...

Tuscan Tomato and Bread Salad (page 144). Another old family favourite.

TUSCAN TOMATO AND BREAD SALAD

La Panzanella

SERVES 6

As a child, when we made this for our lunch whilst out on a summer fishing trip, we would dunk the bread into the sea to soak it. The trick is to squeeze the water out of the bread without destroying the slices completely. You can alter the quantities of tomatoes and basil to suit your own taste.

●

400 g (14 oz) coarse bread, sliced
175 g (6 oz) fresh ripe tomatoes, skinned, seeded and coarsely chopped
100 g (4 oz) red onion, chopped
75 g (3 oz) fresh basil leaves, torn into shreds
8 tablespoons olive oil
salt and freshly milled black pepper

●

METHOD

Wrap the bread in a clean cloth and dunk it in cold, fresh water. Squeeze the water out of the bread, keeping the bread in relatively whole slices. Arrange the slices in the bottom of a salad bowl. Mix the chopped tomatoes and onion together. Spoon over the bread in a thick layer. Scatter the basil on top, then drizzle with the olive oil. Season with salt and pepper. Leave to stand for up to 10 minutes before serving.

RICE SALAD

Insalata di Riso

SERVES 6

You can vary this salad enormously according to what vegetables you want to add. This is the basic format, to which you can add chopped anchovies, flaked tuna, olives, gherkins, capers or cubed cheese – the possibilities are endless.

●

300 g (11 oz) long-grain rice
2 carrots, boiled and cubed
150 g (5 oz) green beans, boiled, topped, tailed and cubed
3 small potatoes, boiled and cubed
3 tomatoes, seeded and cubed
2 tablespoons chopped fresh flatleaf parsley
6 tablespoons olive oil
2 tablespoons lemon juice
salt and freshly milled black pepper

●

METHOD

Boil the rice in salted water for about 15 minutes or until tender. Tip into a sieve or colander then wash and drain it under running water before transferring it into a salad bowl. Add all the cooked vegetables, tomatoes and parsley and mix thoroughly. Add the olive oil and lemon juice, then mix again. Season with salt and pepper and serve.

GREEN BEAN AND EGG SALAD

Insalata di Fagiolini e Uova Sode

SERVES 6

A really very simple salad, the balsamic vinegar is alternative to the more traditional dressing which uses lemon juice.

●

225 g (8 oz) fine green beans, topped and tailed
3 eggs, hard-boiled and shelled
4 spring onions, finely chopped
3 teaspoons balsamic vinegar
8 tablespoons olive oil
salt and freshly milled black pepper

●

METHOD

Boil the beans in plenty of salted water for a few minutes until tender but still crisp. Drain and cool, then arrange in a salad bowl. Chop the hard-boiled eggs and scatter on top. Add the spring onions. Mix the balsamic vinegar with the olive oil and season with salt and pepper. Drizzle this all over the salad and toss together before serving.

Green Bean and Egg Salad: a salad that makes a perfect first course.

CHICKEN SALAD

Insalata di Pollo

SERVES 6

If you happen to have some left-over cooked chicken, this is a marvellous opportunity to use it up. To be truthful, the quantities in this colourful salad vary according to availability and personal preference, so feel free to add or subtract as you like.

●

2 potatoes, boiled and cubed
1 beetroot, boiled and peeled, then cubed
1 cupful of cooked peas
150 g (5 oz) fine green beans, boiled and cubed
2 carrots, cubed
1 short cucumber, peeled and cubed
2 chicken breasts, cooked and cubed
5 tablespoons mayonnaise
2 tablespoons lemon juice
salt and freshly milled black pepper

TO GARNISH
lettuce leaves
cucumber slices

●

METHOD

Mix all the cooked vegetables together, then mix in the cucumber and the chicken breasts. Add the mayonnaise, lemon juice, salt and pepper. Mix together again thoroughly and chill until required. Arrange on a platter to serve, garnished with slices of cucumber and lettuce leaves.

SEAFOOD AND RICE SALAD

Insalata di Mare con Riso

SERVES 6

Use only the freshest possible seafood to make this a salad you will remember for all the right reasons! Don't use seafood preserved in brine or vinegar.

●

300 g (11 oz) long-grain rice
300 g (11 oz) mixed shelled cooked seafood, such as
mussels, prawns, scallops etc.
2 eggs, hard-boiled and shelled
4–6 tablespoons olive oil
2 tablespoons lemon juice
salt and freshly milled black pepper

●

METHOD

Boil the rice in salted water for about 15 minutes until tender, then drain and rinse it under cold running water. Dry the rice thoroughly, then mix it with all the seafood. Mash the hard-boiled eggs and blend thoroughly with the olive oil, lemon juice and salt and pepper. Pour this dressing over the salad and mix together thoroughly. Arrange on a platter and serve.

CHEESE AND ANCHOVY SALAD

Insalata di Formaggio e Acciughe

SERVES 6

Apparently this is a very old recipe for a salad which was enjoyed in Renaissance Florence by none other than Caterina de'Medici herself!

●

450 g (I lb) fresh green salad of any variety: rocket, chicory,
sweet romain etc. or a mixture of more than one type
175 g (6 oz) semi-soft Italian cheese such as Bel Paese
or Provolone, cubed
6 salted anchovy fillets
about 20 salted capers, rinsed, dried and coarsely chopped
6 tablespoons olive oil
freshly milled black pepper

●

METHOD

Wash the salad carefully and dry it thoroughly. Arrange it in a salad bowl. Gently mix in the cheese. Rinse the salted anchovies and dry them carefully, then chop coarsely and mix into the salad leaves. Add the capers and mix together again. Dress with the olive oil and a little pepper, mix once more and serve at once. No salt is added to this recipe, as the anchovies are already salty enough.

CELERIAC SALAD

Insalata di Sedano di Verona

SERVES 6

This salad from Verona in northern Italy has a lovely combination of textures and flavours. It is finished off with a shot of grappa for added bite and interest.

•

300 g (11 oz) celeriac, peeled
150 g (5 oz) Emmenthal, cubed
200 g (7 oz) ham, sliced into strips
2 tablespoons natural yoghurt
4 tablespoons olive oil
1 measure of grappa or aquavit
a large pinch of cinnamon
salt and freshly milled black pepper

•

METHOD

Slice the celeriac into matchsticks, then mix it with the cheese and ham. Add the yoghurt and the olive oil and mix together thoroughly, then add the grappa. Finish off with cinnamon and salt and pepper. Mix everything together very thoroughly. Leave to stand for about 10 minutes and serve.

VEGETABLES

· · · · · · · · · · · · · · · ·

Italy is extremely lucky in that its climate and soil permit literally hundreds of different vegetables to grow all over the country. Out of these precious riches, countless recipes are created either using vegetables as the central ingredient or as one of many other ingredients. Vegetables are often served as a very simple accompaniment to a main course. When this happens they tend to be cooked in the most uncomplicated way: either boiled or fried, with no more than a squeeze of lemon and a drizzle of olive oil to finish them off.

The collection of recipes which follow contains both 'complete meal' vegetable dishes, and some which are designed to accompany the main course. In all cases I have tried to make them recipes which are very simple and easy to cook and shop for, but nevertheless interesting and above all authentically Italian. Do remember that the vegetables should be as fresh as possible for the best results.

STUFFED COURGETTES

Zucchine Ripiene

SERVES 6

For this recipe, the courgettes are filled with a meat stuffing flavoured with Parmesan and nut-meg and stewed in a tomato sauce. Use an apple corer to make the hollow in the courgettes. They are delicious either hot or cold.

●

12 courgettes, washed, topped and tailed
300 g (11 oz) minced veal, beef or pork
2 eggs
175 g (6 oz) freshly grated Parmesan
2–3 tablespoons chopped fresh flatleaf parsley
4 tablespoons fresh breadcrumbs
salt and freshly milled black pepper
a pinch of freshly grated nutmeg
75 g (3 oz) unsalted butter
2 onions, finely chopped
800 g ($1\frac{3}{4}$ lb) canned tomatoes, coarsely chopped

●

METHOD

Boil the courgettes whole in salted water for about 5 minutes or until just tender. Drain and cool. Mix the meat with the eggs, Parmesan, parsley and breadcrumbs. Season with salt, pepper and nutmeg. Core the courgettes and chop the flesh removed from them. Add this to the meat mixture. Replace the inside of the courgettes with the filling mixture. Melt the butter and fry the onions, until transparent. Add the tomatoes and season with salt and pepper. Cover and simmer for about 20 minutes, then slide in the stuffed courgettes. Cover and simmer for a further 20 minutes or until the courgettes are cooked right the way through. Serve hot or cold.

OVERLEAF: Stuffed Courgettes, the best part of this recipe is coring the courgettes.

ROASTED PEPPERS

Peperoni Arrosto

SERVES 6

The pepper is such a deliciously versatile vegetable. You can stuff them with meat, rice or pasta and with a combination of olives, Mozzarella, herbs and capers; they can be added to salads, either raw or cooked; and they can be turned into sauces and soups. With their bright, colourful appearance and their sweet, juicy flavour, they make a welcome contribution to many a table.

●

6 large, juicy peppers, any colours
8 tablespoons olive oil
3 garlic cloves, finely chopped
2 tablespoons chopped fresh parsley
salt and freshly milled black pepper

●

METHOD

Grill the peppers all over until blackened and soft. Wrap them tightly in cling film and leave to cool completely. Then unwrap and remove the exterior transparent skin with a clean scouring pad, or the tips of your fingers dipped in cold water or with light strokes of a sharp knife. Cut in half and remove all the seeds and membranes. Slice them into strips and arrange on a platter. Mix the olive oil and garlic with the parsley. Season generously with salt and pepper, then pour over the peppers. Leave to stand for about 15 minutes, then serve.

BAKED TOMATOES WITH A RICE FILLING

Pomodori Ripieni di Riso

SERVES 6

The taste of these tomatoes always transports me right back to the kitchen of the house where I grew up as a child. I used to hate them with a real passion in those days, but I can remember the exact day when I finally put some in my mouth and discovered that far from being horrible, they were actually delicious! I prefer them cold, but you can have them hot if you prefer them that way. There is plenty of filling, so you need large, tasty tomatoes for this recipe. You can swap this filling mixture for the one used for the stuffed peppers (see page 161) and vice versa.

●

6 large ripe, firm tomatoes, washed and dried
200 g (7 oz) long-grain rice
2 garlic cloves, finely chopped
75 ml (3 fl oz) olive oil
10 leaves fresh basil, torn into shreds
1 tablespoon dried oregano
salt and freshly milled black pepper
1 large potato, cut into 6 thick slices about the same circumference
as the tomatoes

●

METHOD

Pre-heat the oven to 180°C/350°F/gas 4. Slice the tops off the tomatoes and set them aside. Scoop out the inside of the tomatoes and discard the seeds. Chop the flesh of the tomatoes and set aside. Turn the scooped out tomatoes upside down and leave to drain for about 30 minutes. Meanwhile, boil the rice for about 10 minutes in salted water, then drain.

In another pan, gently fry the garlic with the olive oil for about 5 minutes, then stir in the basil and oregano. Mix in the rice and the reserved tomato flesh and season thoroughly with salt and pepper. Use this mixture to fill all the tomatoes and then replace the lids. Oil an ovenproof dish lightly and lay the potato slices on the bottom. Place each tomato on a slice of raw potato and bake in the oven for about 35 minutes or until the rice is tender and the tomatoes soft.

Baked Tomatoes with a Rice Filling (page 157). Perfect either hot or cold.

Stuffed Baked Onions (page 160). Delicious alone or as the perfect accompaniment for game dishes.

STUFFED BAKED ONIONS

Cipolle Ripiene di Magro

SERVES 6

Traditionally served on Christmas Eve in Piedmont, I really love the flavour of this wonderful onion dish; it is somehow so spicy and yet sweet and sour at the some time. You can omit the Mostarda di Frutta *(candied fruits pickled in mustard syrup) if you cannot get hold of it. Most good Italian delicatessens sell it, although some may only stock it nearer to Christmas.*

•

900 ml (1½ pints) water

salt

6 very large onions, peeled

450 g (1 lb) peeled and seeded pumpkin

120 g (4½ oz) Mostarda di Frutta, finely chopped,
and 2–3 tablespoons of its syrup

1 egg, beaten

¼ teaspoon freshly grated nutmeg

175 g (6 oz) amaretti biscuits, crushed

50 g (2 oz) unsalted butter

•

METHOD

Pre-heat the oven to 200°C/400°F/gas 6. Pour the water into a large pan, add the salt and bring to the boil. Drop in the peeled onions and the pumpkin. Boil for about 10 minutes or until the onions are about three-quarters cooked. Take out the onions and place on a perforated tray or a cake rack to drain. Strain the pumpkin very thoroughly, squeeze dry with your hands and then put into a bowl. Add the *Mostarda di Frutta* and syrup, if using, the egg, the nutmeg and amaretti. Mix all this together very thoroughly.

Take the central core out of the onions and discard, leaving a hole through the centre of each onion. Fill each onion with the pumpkin stuffing and level the top. Dot each onion with butter then grease a baking dish thoroughly with the remaining butter and place the stuffed onions in the dish. Bake in the oven for about 40 minutes or until the onions are cooked through. Serve hot or cold.

STUFFED PEPPERS WITH RICE

Peperoni Ripieni di Riso

SERVES 6

This is a deliciously substantial dish which may be eaten either hot or cold and can be served as either as a main course accompanied by a salad or with other vegetable dishes.

•

6 large juicy peppers
300 g (11 oz) long-grain rice
7 tablespoons olive oil
2 tablespoons unsalted butter
2 garlic cloves, crushed
6 salted anchovy fillets, rinsed and chopped
2 tablespoons chopped fresh parsley
salt and freshly milled black pepper
water or vegetable stock for basting

•

METHOD

Pre-heat the oven to 180°C/350°F/gas 4. Roast the peppers under the grill until blackened all over, then wrap them tightly in cling film and leave until cool. Unwrap the peppers and remove their skin completely either with a scouring pad or with a sharp knife, then cut them in half and remove all the seeds and membranes. Boil the rice in lightly salted water until just tender. Drain and tip into a bowl. Heat half the olive oil with the butter and garlic and fry gently until the garlic is completely browned, then discard the garlic. Add the anchovy fillets and parsley to the oil and butter, stir until well combined then pour over the rice. Mix together thoroughly and then fill the halved peppers with rice. Sprinkle with salt and pepper and the remaining olive oil. Cover with foil and bake in the pre-heated oven for about 30 minutes or until tender, basting occasionally with a little water or vegetable stock.

COURGETTES PREPARED IN THE NEAPOLITAN SCAPECE STYLE

Zucchine a Scapece

SERVES 6

This title is pronounced 'ska pay chay'. I always teach my students this dish and although it states quite clearly that you must leave it to stand for a while, or preferably overnight before eating it, it somehow always disappears completely even before the lesson is finished! A perfect treat to serve with pre-dinner drinks.

•

9 large courgettes, topped and tailed
175 ml (6 fl oz) olive oil
a large handful of fresh mint leaves, coarsley chopped
3 garlic cloves, finely chopped
6 tablespoons good quality vinegar
salt

•

METHOD

Cut the courgettes into thin slices lengthways. Place them on a wooden board, cover with a cloth and leave them in the sun to dry out for about 3 hours. Alternatively, place them on baking sheets and place in the oven at 140°C/275°F/gas 1 for about an hour to dry out completely without colouring.

Heat about 10 cm (4 in) of olive oil in a large pan and fry all the dried courgettes, in batches if necessary, until golden. Drain carefully on kitchen paper, then transfer them into a dish and sprinkle with the mint, garlic, vinegar and salt. Cover and leave to stand for about 4 hours in a cool place or, even better, overnight.

Courgettes Prepared in the Scapece Style: delicious nibbles to serve with an aperitif.

BAKED FENNEL WITH CHEESE

Finocchi alla Parmigiana

SERVES 6

Fontina is a cheese that is used extensively in Italian cooking. If Fontina is unavailable, use Bel Paese or Gruyère instead, but be sure to use a cheese with an intense flavour.

●

6 fennel bulbs, trimmed and cleaned
150 g (5 oz) Fontina
50 g (2 oz) unsalted butter
$\frac{1}{4}$ teaspoon freshly grated nutmeg
salt

●

METHOD

Pre-heat the oven to 200°C/400°F/gas 6. Quarter the fennel bulbs and boil them in salted water until tender. Drain thoroughly. Slice the Fontina into strips. Butter an ovenproof dish and arrange one layer of fennel across the bottom. Scatter a layer of Fontina over the fennel and sprinkle with nutmeg. Dot with half the remaining butter. Cover with a second layer of fennel and dot with the rest of the butter, then cover with the remaining Fontina strips. Bake in the pre-heated oven for about 20 minutes or until the top is browned and bubbling hot.

BAKED COURGETTE MOULD

Tortino di Zucchine

SERVES 6

This is the best way to marry the flavours of fresh, ripe summer tomatoes and courgettes. This recipe makes a really good main course or a fairly substantial first course dish.

•

8–10 medium to large courgettes, topped, tailed and sliced
into thick tongues
salt
4 tablespoons plain white flour
250 ml (8 fl oz) sunflower oil
3 tablespoons olive oil
1 onion, chopped
800 g (1¾ lb) ripe summer tomatoes, skinned, seeded and coarsely chopped
8 leaves fresh basil, torn into shreds
a large pinch of dried oregano
salt and freshly milled black pepper
150 g (5 oz) Mozzarella, finely chopped

•

METHOD

Lay the courgette 'tongues' in a colander. Sprinkle with salt and cover with a plate. Weigh the plate down and stand the colander in a sink to drain for about 2 hours. Rinse and dry the courgettes, then toss lightly in plain flour. Heat the sunflower oil until a small piece of bread dropped into the oil sizzles instantly. Fry the courgettes, in batches, until golden brown then drain thoroughly on kitchen paper. Heat the olive oil and fry the onion until very soft, then add the tomatoes, basil and oregano. Stir together and season. Cover and simmer for about 30 minutes, then sieve the sauce. Pre-heat the oven to 180°C/350°F/gas 4. Cover the bottom of an ovenproof dish with a layer of sieved sauce. Cover with a layer of fried courgettes, then with a layer of Mozzarella. Cover with another layer of sauce, more courgettes and more Mozzarella. Continue in this way until all the ingredients have been used up. Bake in the oven for about 20 minutes or until heated through.

BAKED AUBERGINE MOULD

Tortino di Melanzane al Forno

SERVES 6 GENEROUSLY

A very filling dish, this contains lots of eggs which bind the aubergines into a kind of savoury herb-flavoured cake. Serve it with a light salad.

•

6 large aubergines, washed and dried
salt
6 tablespoons plain white flour
250 ml (8 fl oz) sunflower or olive oil
12 eggs, beaten
2 tablespoons chopped fresh parsley
1 teaspoon dried marjoram
salt and freshly milled black pepper
oil for greasing

•

METHOD

Slice the aubergines in 1 cm ($\frac{1}{2}$ in) thick slices and lay them in a colander. Sprinkle generously with salt and cover with a plate. Put a weight on the plate and leave the aubergines to drain for about 2 hours. Rinse and dry carefully. Heat the sunflower or olive oil until a small piece of bread dropped into it sizzles instantly. Dip the dry aubergine slices in the flour and fry them all on both sides until golden brown. Drain very thoroughly on kitchen paper. Pre-heat the oven to 190°C/375°F/gas 5. Whisk the herbs into the beaten eggs and season them with salt and pepper.

Arrange the aubergines in an ovenproof dish then pour over the egg mixture. Shake the dish to distribute the egg throughout the aubergines and then bake in the oven for about 15 minutes or until just set. Serve at once.

PAN-FRIED MUSHROOMS

Funghetti in Padella

SERVES 4–6

This method of cooking mushrooms suits any kind of mushroom you might choose, either wild or cultivated.

●

750 g (1½ lb) fresh mushrooms, trimmed
2 garlic cloves, finely chopped
4 tablespoons olive oil
3 tablespoons chopped fresh flatleaf parsley
salt and freshly milled black pepper

●

METHOD

Slice the mushrooms thinly. Fry the garlic in the olive oil over a gentle heat until completely soft, then add the mushrooms. Stir together thoroughly and cover. Allow the mushrooms to exude all their liquid, and then re-absorb it. Sprinkle with the parsley, season with salt and pepper and stir. Cook for a further 5 minutes, then serve at once.

DESSERTS

· · · · · · · · · · · · · · ·

Our final chapter covers the sweet course: dulcis in fundo. Many people I know tell me that they don't really feel like they've had a complete meal unless they finish off on a sweet note. I am also fascinated by people in restaurants who refuse a first course because they prefer puddings to starters. Personally, if I am out at a restaurant I am far too weak-willed to have such thoughts!

This selection of desserts is not too naughty, although some are less virtuous than others! But they are all, without question, very easy to put together and equally good to eat. Traditionally, in Italy, desserts are reserved for special occasions, and the meal is otherwise finished off with fruit. Quite a few of these very simple sweets are actually served to children for afternoon tea, but I think they are so good that the whole family should share them.

POACHED SPICED PEARS AND APPLES

Pere e Mele Cotte con le Spezie

SERVES 6

I think what makes this dessert very special is to chill the cooked fruit and then to serve it with a little lightly sweetened, very cold whipped cream. Alternatively, after chilling, tip a table-spoonful of your favourite liqueur over the fruit or serve with warm custard.

•

4 firm pears, peeled, cored and quartered
4 firm dessert apples (russets or cox's, for example), peeled,
cored and quartered
4 tablespoons cold water
$\frac{1}{2}$ cinnamon stick
2 cloves
a pinch of freshly grated nutmeg
pared zest of 1 lemon
5 tablespoons caster sugar

•

METHOD

Place all the pear and apple quarters in a pan with all the remaining ingredients. Cover and simmer very gently for about 10 minutes, shaking the pan occasionally, until the fruit is completely soft. Transfer into a bowl and cool.

Remove the lemon zest, cinnamon stick and cloves. Chill the fruit and serve on its own or with cream, ice cream or topped with a shot of your favourite Italian liqueur such as Amaretto, Strega or Galliano.

OVERLEAF: Venetian Fritters (page 172). Light and fluffy, studdied with candied fruits, these fritters only need a dusting of sugar and they are ready for Carnevale!

VENETIAN FRITTERS

Frittelle Venete

These traditional, sweet fritters used to be cooked and sold to passers-by during carnival time in Venice. The batter needs to rise before cooking, so plan ahead a little for this one.

●

MAKES ABOUT 28 FRITTERS

120 g ($4\frac{1}{2}$ oz) sultanas, soaked in tepid water for about 10 minutes,
then drained and dried

1 measure anise or rum

450 g (1 lb) plain white flour, sifted

75 g (3 oz) caster sugar

35 g ($1\frac{1}{2}$ oz) fresh yeast

about 250 ml (8 fl oz) warm milk

a pinch of salt

50 g (2 oz) pine kernels

50 g (2 oz) chopped candied peel

grated zest of 1 lemon

900 ml ($1\frac{1}{2}$ pints) sunflower or olive oil

TO SERVE

icing sugar

●

METHOD

Cover the sultanas with the anise or rum and set aside to soak. Put the flour in a bowl with the sugar. Dilute the yeast in a little of the warm milk. Make a hole in the centre of the flour and pour in the yeast mixture. Mix thoroughly, adding enough milk to make a smooth, soft dough. Mix in the sultanas, salt, pine kernels, candied peel and lemon zest. Cover and leave to rise in a warm spot for about 6 hours.

Mix the dough again and add more milk to make it wet enough to spoon. Heat the oil in a deep pan until a cube of bread dropped into it sizzles instantly. Fry the fritters in batches, dropping the dough into the hot oil by the tablespoon. As soon as the fritter returns to the surface, scoop it out and allow it to drain. Sprinkle with icing sugar and serve hot with a chilled dessert wine or ice cream.

PANETTONE WITH ICE CREAM

Panettone al Gelato

SERVES 6

Probably the most delicious and the most simple of all Italian desserts! You can buy Panettone at Italian delicatessens, especially at Christmas time. There are lots of flavours of Panettone so just choose whichever one you like.

●

1 x 450 g (1 lb) Panettone
450 g (1 lb) best quality ice cream: vanilla, chocolate chip, nougat,
chocolate or hazelnut flavour

●

METHOD

Cut the top off the *Panettone* and scoop out most of the inside, leaving a relatively thick border all the way around the edges and the bottom. You can use the extra *Panettone* for another recipe. Allow the ice cream to soften to a spreading consistency. Fill the *Panettone* completely with ice cream, then replace the top. Place in the freezer until about 15 minutes before you want to eat, then slice into wedges and serve.

OVERLEAF: Panettone with Ice Cream. One very simple solution to make all that Christmas cooking a little bit less like hard work!

DAL 1860

Negli archivi della casa Lazzaroni si conservano ricette originali di panettone: le più antiche risalgono al 1860, quando Davide Lazzaroni confezionava il suo rinomato "Panalloue" –servando lo tipira pronuncia lombarda–, che comparivano avvolto nel suo prezioso incarto, con la caratteristica etichetta, nei caffè, nei ritrovi, nelle dimore patrizie tutto il m

MASCARPONE WITH PEARS

Mascarpone con le Pere

SERVES 6

There is a proverb in Italy which roughly translated means: 'Don't let the farmer know how good his pears taste with Mascarpone'. The two together make a truly marvellous combination. If you like, you can poach the pears and cool them, then serve with the cheese. Use as much or as little cheese as you like, especially if you are watching the calories.

●

6 large ripe pears, peeled, cored and quartered
juice of $\frac{1}{2}$ lemon
12 tablespoons Mascarpone

TO GARNISH
shelled walnuts

●

METHOD

Arrange the quartered pears in a circle on a dish and brush them very lightly with lemon juice to prevent them going brown. Whip the cheese to make it smooth and light, if necessary with a tablespoon of cold milk, then pile it into the centre of the dish. Garnish with the walnuts and serve.

TIRAMISU WITH FRUIT

Tiramisú alla Frutta

S E R V E S   6

In this case the fruit is strawberries, but any soft fruit or peaches or apricots works equally well.

●

5 egg yolks

5 tablespoons caster sugar

$\frac{1}{2}$ teaspoon vanilla essence

6 tablespoons white rum

400 g (14 oz) Mascarpone

450 g (1 lb) ripe strawberries

3 egg whites, chilled

3 tablespoons whipped cream

10 hard amaretti biscuits, roughly crumbled

about 25 boudoir biscuits or savoiardi or sponge fingers

200 ml (7 fl oz) apple juice

●

M E T H O D

Beat the egg yolks with a whisk until pale yellow and fluffy, gradually adding all the caster sugar as you beat. Add the vanilla essence and 1 tablespoon of white rum. Stir the Mascarpone cheese with a fork to soften it as much as possible. Gently stir the Mascarpone into the egg yolk mixture. Cut about a quarter of the strawberries into very small pieces and tip them and all their juice into the egg and Mascarpone mixture. Beat the egg whites until stiff, then fold in. Do the same with the whipped cream. Add about one-third of the crumbled amaretti biscuits to the mixture, folding them in gently. Mix the remaining rum with the apple juice. Slice all the remaining strawberries and put a few to one side. Dip some of the biscuits into the apple juice and rum mixture, just enough biscuits to cover the bottom of a pretty glass dish. Arrange a layer of strawberries over the biscuits, then cover with a layer of the Mascarpone cream. Repeat until the dish is filled, finishing with a layer of Mascarpone cream, then decorate with the remaining amaretti biscuits and the reserved strawberries. Chill for at least 5 hours, preferably overnight, before serving.

Tiramisu with Fruit (page 177). Carefully layered, this dessert is lighter than you would imagine.

Italian Fruit Salad (page 180). My favourite picture – what could be more delcious than fresh fruit?

ITALIAN FRUIT SALAD

Macedonia

SERVES 6

An Italian fruit salad is always different to a fruit salad from any other part of the world, mainly because the fruit is always cut into such small pieces and it is always (unless children are going to eat it) finished off with a little measure of a liqueur or spirit. The fruit used varies according to what is in season.

●

2 small dessert apples, peeled, cored and quartered
5 plums, quartered and stoned
2 peaches, peeled, quartered and stoned
5 apricots, peeled, quartered and stoned
2 small pears, peeled, cored and quartered
juice of 1 lemon
4 tablespoons caster sugar
6 tablespoons sweet vermouth or liqueur

●

METHOD

Cut all the fruit into small pieces and cover it with lemon juice. Mix it together with the sugar and the vermouth or liqueur. Mix very thoroughly, then chill until required. Serve with sweetened whipped cream or ice cream, or just on its own.

DAISY CAKE

Torta Margherita

This is the most classic of all Italian cakes, delicious with a glass of dessert wine at the end of a meal. You can also use this simple cake to make a variety of other desserts – for example, slice it in half lengthways and fill it with whipped cream and raspberries.

●

MAKES 1 X 25 CM (10 IN) CAKE

6 eggs, separated

100 g (4 oz) plain white flour, sifted

50 g (2 oz) cornflour, sifted

200 g (7 oz) unsalted butter, melted and cooled

$\frac{1}{2}$ tablespoon grated lemon zest

a pinch of salt

butter for greasing

plain flour for dusting

icing sugar for dusting

●

METHOD

Pre-heat the oven to 180°C/350°F/gas 4 and grease and flour a 25 cm (10 in) cake tin. Beat the egg yolks until pale yellow, then gradually beat in the flour and corn-flour. Gradually beat in the butter, lemon zest and salt. Whisk the egg whites into stiff peaks then fold into the mixture. Pour the mixture into the prepared cake tin and bake in the pre-heated oven for about 40 minutes or until a clean knife inserted into the centre of the cake comes out completely clean. Cool in the cake tin, then turn out on to a rack. Dust with icing sugar to serve.

APRICOT CROSTINI

Crostini all'Albicocca

SERVES 6

Crostini are very popular and fashionable these days, although one does not often come across sweet crostini! They are also delicious made with very sweet, ripe, soft pears, or even ripe bananas.

●

12 ripe, soft apricots
300 g (11 oz) Ricotta
12 slices Italian bread, walnut bread is especially good for this dish
4 tablespoons clear honey

●

METHOD

Remove the stones from the apricots then purée them in a food processor. Mix them with the Ricotta. Toast the bread lightly and spread with honey. Pile the apricot mixture on top of the slices of toast and serve.

Apricot Crostini: Ripe apricots, fresh Ricotta and scented honey make these crostini irresistible.

PEACHES STUFFED WITH MARZIPAN

Pesche Ripiene al Marzapane

SERVES 6

This is a wonderful way to use up the last peaches of the season.

●

6 large, dry, end-of-season peaches, washed and dried

3 tablespoons marzipan, softened

2 tablespoons coarsely chopped cooking chocolate

2 tablespoons coarsely chopped blanched almonds

2 tablespoons caster sugar

2 tablespoons sweet dessert wine

$\frac{1}{2}$ teaspoon ground cinnamon

1 tumbler dry white wine

sugar for dusting

biscuits crumbs for dusting

●

METHOD

Pre-heat the oven to 180°C/350°F/gas 4. Halve the peaches and remove the stones. Scoop out a little of the flesh to leave a smooth, even hollow in the centre of each peach. Do not perforate the peach or the filling will ooze out while cooking. Mash the peach flesh with the marzipan, chocolate, almonds, sugar, dessert wine and cinnamon. Pack this mixture evenly into each peach and arrange the filled peaches neatly in a baking dish. Pour the white wine around them and sprinkle with sugar and biscuit crumbs. Cover loosely with foil and bake for about 30 minutes or until soft. Serve warm or cold.

RICOTTA CREAM WITH CANTUCCINI BISCUITS

Dolce di Ricotta con i Cantuccini

SERVES 6

Ricotta is used a great deal in both sweet and savoury Italian recipes. Here is a very simple idea. Cantuccini biscuits can be bought at all good Italian delicatessens. They are very hard, nutty almond biscuits which can also be served on their own and dunked into a glass of chilled dessert wine for a really marvellous end to a meal.

●

500 g (1$\frac{1}{4}$lb) very fresh Ricotta or cream cheese
75 g (3 oz) icing sugar, sifted
4 egg yolks
6 tablespoons dark rum
1$\frac{1}{2}$ tablespoons Marsala wine
300 ml (10 fl oz) whipping cream, whipped until fairly stiff

TO SERVE
Cantuccini biscuits

●

METHOD

If you are using cream cheese instead of Ricotta, whip it to give it a lighter texture. Mix together the Ricotta or whipped cream cheese, icing sugar and egg yolks until you have a light, smoothly blended mixture. Stir in the rum and Marsala, then carefully fold in the whipped cream. Pour the mixture into individual bowls or stemmed glasses and chill for 3 hours. Remove from the refrigerator just before serving with some Cantuccini biscuits.

ITALIAN MENUS

Here are some menu ideas that balance both the flavour, texture and appearance of the dishes. You can, of course, add or subtract whatever you wish, according to your appetite or the occasion. In those menus where I have not suggested a dessert, I have taken it upon myself to decide that it was not actually necessary! You may disagree with me and decide to add a favourite of your own or one from the book or, as would happen in Italy, serve fresh fruit. I have also sometimes suggested an accompanying vegetable, a simple green, mixed or tomato salad, or boiled or mashed potatoes – to make the meal more complete. All of these suggestions are in *italic*.

1 A SPRING LUNCH
Rice and Peas (page 33)
Baked Fish on a Bed of Rosemary,
Potatoes and Garlic (page 105)
Italian Fruit Salad (page 180)

2 A SPRINGTIME MENU
Risotto with Parsley (page 29)
Stewed Minute Steak (page 68)
Mashed potatoes and a steamed or boiled green vegetable dressed with olive oil and lemon juice

3 AN EARLY SUMMER SUNDAY LUNCH
Make this when cauliflower is cheap
and plentiful.
Cauliflower Soup (page 20)
Devilled Chicken (page 84)
Panettone with Ice Cream (page 173)

4 A SIMPLE SUMMER SUPPER
Tomato Soup (served chilled if you
want to) (page 15)
Grilled Steak with Balsamic Vinegar
(page 78)
Pan-fried Mushrooms (page 167)
Tiramisu with Fruit (page 177)

5 A SUMMER SUPPER
Easy Minestrone (page 16)
Simple Beef Olives (page 72)
Green salad
Boiled potatoes dressed with olive oil
Mascarpone with Pears (page 176)

6 A COLOURFUL MENU FOR SUMMERTIME
Pasta with Yellow Pepper Sauce
(page 53)
Prawns in a Tomato Sauce (page 112)
Mixed salad
Fresh peaches

7 DELICIOUSLY TANGY SUMMER MENU
Pasta with Pesto (page 48)
Lemon-flavoured Meatballs (page 73)
Warm steamed spinach dressed with olive oil and lemon juice
Ricotta Cream *with fresh strawberries and Cantuccini Biscuits* (page 185)

8 AN IDEAL SUMMERTIME MENU
Stuffed Peppers with Rice (page 161)
Stuffed Courgettes (page 153)
Mascarpone with Pears (page 176)

9 A SEASONAL MENU

Mackerel is in season from November through to early summer.

Easy Chick Pea Soup (page 18)
Mackerel with White Wine and
Tomatoes (page 101)
Apricot Crostini (page 182)

10 AN AUTUMN SUPPER

You can eat the dessert with your fingers if you want to.

Rice in a Clear Chicken Soup (page 25)
Simple Stew (page 64)
Venetian Fritters (page 172)

11 AN AUTUMN FEAST, REFLECTING THE COLOURS OF THE SEASON

Rice and Pumpkin (page 30)
Red Mullet with Cured Ham
(page 113)
Steamed carrots dressed with olive oil
Blood orange salad

12 A WINTERY TREAT

Red Onion Soup (page 26)
Grilled Fish (page 104)
Baked Fennel with Cheese (page164)
Daisy Cake (page 181)

13 FOR CHILLY WINTER NIGHTS

Potato Soup (page 24) with Crostini for
Soup (page 17)
Meatballs in Parma Ham (page 76)
Poached Spiced Pears and Apples *served*
with warm custard (page 169)

14 GOOD FOR A WINTER SUNDAY LUNCH

Pasta with a Spinach Sauce (page 56)
Simple Stew (page 64)
Daisy Cake *filled with whipped cream*
and ripe bananas (page 181)

15 WINTER WARMER

Pasta with Garlic, Tomato and Basil
Sauce (page 46)
Lamb Casserole with Peas (page 69)
Fresh pears with Dolcelatte

16 MULTI-SEASONAL RECIPE

Depending upon the season, you can vary the vegetables used in the soup.

Vegetable Soup (page 21)
Pot-roasted Pork in Milk (page 77)
Daisy Cake (page 181)

17 FISH SUPPER

Simple Fish Casserole (page 117)
Cheese and Anchovy Salad (page 150)
Mascarpone with Pears (page 176)

18 FOR VEGETARIANS

Non-fish eaters leave out the tuna.

Pasta with Mushroom and Tuna Sauce
(page 52)
Baked Courgette Mould (page 165)
Peaches Stuffed with Marzipan
(page 184)

19 VEGETARIAN LUNCH

Pasta with Courgettes (page 50)
Stuffed Baked Onions (page 160)
Mixed seasonal salad

20 VEGETARIAN SUPPER

Easy Bean Soup (page 22)
Baked Tomatoes with a Rice Filling
(page 157)
Poached Spiced Pears and Apples
(page 169)

21 FOR FISH-EATING VEGETARIANS

Make sure you use vegetable stock.

Parsley Risotto (page 29)
Cod Fillets with Lemon Juice and
White Wine (page 108)
Tomato salad
Italian Fruit Salad (page 180)

22 LOW FAT, LOW CALORIE DELICIOUS SUPPER

Pasta with Fat-free Tomato Sauce
(page 44)
Poached Chicken (page 93)
Grilled Vegetable Salad (page 141)
Italian Fruit Salad (page 180)

23 COMFORT FOOD WITH PLENTY OF BODY!

Clear Chicken Soup with Pastina
(page 25)
Chicken with Peppers (page 81)
Peaches Stuffed with Marzipan
(page 184)

24 COMFORTING MENU

Easy Bean Soup (page 22)
Baked Aubergine Mould (page 166)
Green salad

25 FILLING, AND UNMISTAKABLY ITALIAN!

Rice and Lentils (page 37)
Chicken Casserole with Tomato and
Rosemary (page 92)
*A steamed green vegetable dressed with
olive oil*

26 PASTA AND SALAD IS ALWAYS WELCOME

Pasta with a Meat and Tomato Sauce
(page 57)
Salad of Mozzarella, Tomatoes and
Basil (page 140)

27 A COLD SUPPER TO PREPARE IN ADVANCE

Roasted Peppers (page 156)
Hard-boiled Eggs Stuffed with Tuna
(page 128)
Green salad
Tiramisu with Fruit (page 177)

28 AN EASY SUPPER

Most of which can be prepared in advance.

Seafood and Rice Salad (page 149)
Mini Omelettes with Tomato Sauce
(page 125)
Green salad

29 LIGHT SUPPER MENU

Eggs in Tomatoes (page 133)
Mascarpone with Pears (page 176)

30 A SIMPLE SUPPER

You can make this more or less filling, according
to appetites.

Cheese and Anchovy Salad (page 150)
Simple Fish Casserole (page 117)
*Green salad dressed with olive oil and
balsamic vinegar*

31 EASY SUPPER

Risotto with Courgettes (page 34)
Poached Trout (page 116)
*Mixed green salad dressed with olive oil
and lemon juice*

32 TASTY SUPPER

Vary the choice of the omelette and you have a
wonderful vegetarian feast. You can easily adjust
the size of the omelettes depending on how
many you want to serve – and how hungry
they are!

Salame Omelette (page 121)
Tuna and Bean Salad (page 137)
Tuscan Tomato and Bread Salad
(page 144)

33 NORTHERN ITALIAN LUNCH
Celeriac Salad (page 151)
Italian Roast Chicken (page 89)
*Warm boiled potatoes, courgettes and
carrots dressed with olive oil*

34 A ROMAN MENU
Chicken Saltimbocca (page 97)
Roasted Peppers (page 156)
Peaches Stuffed with Marzipan
(page 184)

35 A FAVOURITE WITH MY ELDEST SON
Tomato Soup (page 15)
Chicken Breasts with a Cheese Filling
(page 88)
*Steamed green beans dressed with olive oil
and lemon juice*
Venetian Fritters (page 172)

36 SATISFYING AND COLOURFUL
Pasta with Yellow Pepper Sauce
(page 53)
Stewed Minute Steak with a Garlic and
Tomato Sauce (page 68)
*Boiled new potatoes dressed with olive oil
and chopped herbs*
Green salad with rocket

37 LUNCH OR SUPPER MENU
For a hungry family of gourmets!
Pasta with a Fish Sauce (page 49)
Escalopes with Lemon and Herbs
(page 61)
*Steamed courgettes dressed with olive oil
and lemon juice*
Ricotta Cream with Cantuccini Biscuits
(page 185)

38 FOUR VERY FILLING COURSES
*You can cut one omelette into six portions when
served with these other filling dishes.*
Potato and Chicken Liver Omelette
(page 124)
Rice and Cabbage (page 32)
Chicken Salad (page 48)
Venetian Fritters with ice cream
(page 172)

39 THE FULL MENU!
*Sometimes you can serve the full four courses:
antipasto, pasta or risotto, meat and vegetables,
plus dessert.*
Courgettes Prepared in the Scapece
Style (page 162)
Pasta with Sun-dried Tomatoes (page
45) OR Tomato Risotto (page 38)
Escalopes with White Wine and
Orange (page 65)
*A warm, green steamed vegetable dressed
with lemon juice and olive oil*
Warm Daisy Cake *with a warm
chocolate sauce* (page 181)

40 BUFFET PARTY MENU FOR 60
Multiply all recipes by 10.
Rice Salad (page 145)
Green Bean and Egg Salad (page 146)
Chicken Salad (page 148)
Salame Omelette (page 121)
Cold Spinach Omelette (page 132)
Pasta with Pesto (page 48)
Pasta with a Yellow Pepper Sauce
(page 53)
Mascarpone with Pears (page 176)
Ricotta Cream *with fresh strawberries*
(page 185)

INDEX